## WHAT OTHERS ARE SAYING ABOUT

"Melissa Giovagnoli's book is a gold mine of information to college students about how to start building their professional network for a successful career. Melissa shows you that the people who can really help you build a successful career are right at your fingertips. LinkedIn is the best way to take the first steps to establish your professional network, which you will continue to use throughout your career. The real-life examples that Melissa and John describe, plus LinkedIn screens to illustrate their points, makes it easy to get started. Whether you're new to LinkedIn or using it already, I highly recommend *Graduate to LinkedIn.*"

**Jan Wallen**

Author of *Mastering LinkedIn in 7 Days or Less* and Creator of LinkedIn Works!

www.LinkedInWorks.com

LinkedIn – www.linkedin.com/in/janwallen

"The first section of the book reinforces an essential state of mind on social and professional relationships – Networlding. The second section offers the best guidance towards Linkedin effectiveness in a Networlding perspective. This book is a must read for any grad student and an amazing new approach to the world of professional networks!"

**Pedro Caramez**

pt.linkedin.com/in/caramez

LinkedIn Author, Trainer & Consultant

Linked Portugal – www.linkedportugal.com

"*Graduate to LinkedIn* is a must-read not just for college graduates, but for anyone seeking to make solid, fruitful, and long-lasting connections on line. The authors, in an easily accessible step-by-step format, provide absolutely essential information on identifying, initiating and developing key career building relationships on LinkedIn. If you want to skyrocket your career with integrity, I highly recommend that you read this book."

**Brenda Bernstein**

Owner and Senior Editor, The Essay Expert LLC

www.TheEssayExpert.com

Author of *LinkedIn Power Tune-Up: 18 Expert Tips for a Highly Effective LinkedIn Profile*

*Books and More that Make the World Better*

**www.Networlding.com**

First Networlding Publishing edition 2010

Cover Design by Michelle Alicino
Interior Design by Katie Nordt

# Graduate to LinkedIn

JUMP-START YOUR CAREER NETWORK NOW

John Fowler

Melissa Giovagnoli Wilson

# Contents

# Foreword

**JOHN** — Just recently I was sitting in my home office with my MacBook, listening to my favorite band on iTunes; within the browser, Gmail, Twitter, and LinkedIn vied for my attention. I was working on a LinkedIn workshop for a client and furiously brainstorming for unique ways to emphasize the importance of mutually beneficial relationships — online or offline. I needed some inspiration, so I pulled from my book collection one of my favorite resources, *Networlding: Building Relationships and Opportunities for Success*, a book by Melissa Giovagnoli Wilson and Jocelyn Carter-Miller. "I wonder if the authors of this book are on Twitter?" I thought. That would be cool. Sure enough, I found Melissa, AKA @Networlding, and sent her a tweet about my favorite book on networking.

Not even two days later, I received a call on my iPhone from Melissa asking me if I wanted to meet to discuss collaborating on a project. I couldn't believe how quickly our conversation had progressed. Before I knew it, I was presented with an opportunity to partner with a best-selling author, the president of an amazing consultancy to write this very book. I was thrilled, humbled, and flattered. This opportunity was a no-brainer — a chance to contribute to something that would utilize skills and passions I had been growing for the past several years of my career. How did she know I was the right person she was looking for? How did she know I had experience with leveraging the power of LinkedIn? How did she know that I had a knack for using social networking platforms to initiate and foster meaningful relationships?

Of course, the answer is LinkedIn. Twitter allowed me to be found, but LinkedIn allowed Melissa to assess my knowledge, abilities, and experiences. It revealed my professional brand — who I was and who I aspired to be. It served as a platform for both of us to initiate, build, and nurture a business partnership. And as I write this book — I'm almost 30 years old — It makes me all the more curious about how things would have been different if I had access to these types of opportunities in college. The key word here is *access*. The value of relationships hasn't changed since I was in college. Integrity. Loyalty. Cooperation. These things will never change. What *has* changed are the technologies; now more than ever, they enable us to connect with people who can help us lead more fulfilling careers.

To most of you reading this book, social networking platforms are nothing new. Whether it be YouTube, Twitter, Facebook or something else; whichever collaborative tools you use, we challenge you to apply your existing skills to a different space. We dare you to join the largest business network online and begin building your professional network *before* you earn your degree. More than anything, it's our hope that you are empowered by this book to take early ownership of your career by understanding the process of building meaningful relationships, whether it's in person, on LinkedIn, or on some other social network.

**MELISSA** — When I saw that John had been promoting Networlding through Twitter, I of course searched for him on LinkedIn. There I found he was working on a LinkedIn workshop, and I also saw that he was in the age group — 12 through 29 — that had been the focus of my philanthropy for the last decade through my organization Leadership 12 through 29.

I started teaching networking over fifteen years ago and have found LinkedIn to be the best tool for business networking I have ever used. Then here was John in the demographic range where I focused my philanthropic efforts, very adept and also committed to using LinkedIn for his career development and success; it just made sense to connect with John to learn more about how he was using LinkedIn.

Having been in business for more than two decades, I'm wise enough to know that people aren't always as great as they first appear. So when I talked with John and he immediately was open to meeting, had actually read my book, and, even better, actually used the ideas in it to improve his career, I said, "John, if you are open to it, let's work on a book called 'Graduate to LinkedIn' and let's give a portion of our earnings to help kids who need support getting a good start in life."

John was on board from the very start. Within a week of our meeting he did what I tell all of those I help author books do — he researched Amazon for similar books (there weren't other exact books, but plenty of books growing on the subject of LinkedIn training), and compared those books to one another, noting both the favorable and not-so-favorable aspects of each.

He did a superb job gathering everything we needed to offer — the best strategies, tips and tactics for our readers. He interviewed dozens of college students and recent grads. Along the way, he also managed to highlight the heart of the Networlding process: what we value determines what we achieve. If you don't give your dreams real value in your everyday life, you'll never reach them.

But perhaps the best thing about getting connected to John is that he thinks I'm doing *him* a favor. On the contrary, after ten years of training, coaching and facilitating the process I co-created with Jocelyn Carter Miller called Networlding, I know that this will benefit the readers infinitely more than it will John. Above everything else, I value making a difference; I wouldn't have worked on this book if it didn't make one. If this book allows me to help young professionals get great starts in life, I will be overjoyed.

So please, prove me right. Are you ready? Let's begin!

# Acknowledgments

**JOHN** — My deepest thanks to the many people who helped me create this book, and also to the members of my career support network, who have all played an integral role in my development as a professional and as a person: Melissa Giovagnoli, Bob Dean, Eddie Turner, Jonathan Eisler, Chetan Borkhetaria, Dustin Williams, Julie Bechtold, Ilianna Kwaske, Katie Andrien, Janny Vincent, Sarah Riahi, Stephanie Laguens, Sid Chapon, Gilbert Melott; to all the great students who contributed success stories, all my beloved friends from St. Louis and Kansas City, my sisters, my parents, my girlfriend Marie, and of course, God.

**MELISSA** — Thank you to all the many Networlding fans who have been part of Networlding since it began a decade ago. Thank you Jocelyn nurturing the idea of Networlding all these years. Thank you to all the many folks in Chicago like Tom Johnson, Dan Lyne, Ty Tabing, Bob Dean, Eddie Turner, Sarah Miller Caldicott and more who are working to create the Networlding Innovation and Collaboration Center that will have a deep focus on helping college grads get great starts in their careers. Thank you, finally, to my great family and friends who are always cheering me on with my dreams.

# Purpose of this Book

The purpose of this book is to help you understand that the people who can best help you build a successful career are right at your fingertips. It may seem that LinkedIn was created solely for experienced professionals interested in networking and conducting business. But the truth is, LinkedIn is the perfect tool you, as tomorrow's leaders, can use to establish a professional brand and launch a professional network. This network is what we call a career support network — a web of meaningful connections just keystrokes away from helping you get that first job upon graduation.

Our intention is to provide you with a guide for using the most powerful social networking tool of all. By picking up this book, you have already taken the first step toward jump-starting your career. We will walk you through the Networlding approach to LinkedIn, a practical and proven process for finding and connecting with the people who could play an significant part in your development as a successful young professional, emerging leader, or entrepreneur. Using the Networlding approach results in the formation of meaningful connections with influencers and mentors — people who help you grow as a professional and get the job you really want.

In order to write this book, we interviewed dozens of students and recent graduates about their experiences using LinkedIn. This was no easy task because most of the students we contacted did not have a LinkedIn profile and if they did have one, they weren't sure exactly how to use it. In the end, however, we were fortunate enough to connect with close to 20 students and new grads (undergraduate and graduate) who had experienced success with LinkedIn. It was these individuals who contributed the insights and stories that made this book possible.

Although we were interested in learning about how students were able to use LinkedIn to obtain internships or secure full-time employment, it's important to note that this was only one piece of the puzzle. Landing a job was not the be-all, end-all indication of success. What mattered most were the ways they used LinkedIn to find and connect with people who were willing and able to facilitate their career-building endeavors. It's our hope that these stories inspire you to the point that LinkedIn becomes your go-to resource for creating your own stories of success — stories made possible by following the fulfilling process we call Networlding.

# What's the Deal with LinkedIn?

# What's the Deal with LinkedIn?

Remember *The Tipping Point*, the book that really was one of
the first to offer more insight into the science of networks? One of
Gladwell's signature stories was all about Paul Revere. What would have
happened if Paul Revere hadn't warned the nation that the British were
coming? His success played a pivitol role in how America became the
free country you know it to be, so how did he do it? It didn't happen
because he randomly rode through towns yelling, "The British are coming!" It happened because he intentionally knocked on doors of people
he knew had the ability to spread the word because *they* knew lots of
important people. His friends told their friends, who told their friends,
and before you knew it, the entire American army was ready to defend
its country. Revere *successfully used his network* to accomplish his goal.
Had he been alive today, he may have just sent a mass email, or better
yet, sent his message to all of his trusted connections on LinkedIn.

When you want to communicate something important, like your life
goals for instance, talking to everyone you already know can only get you
so far. You also need to make sure you talk to the *right* people. With that
said, what if you not only had access to everyone you know, but also you
have access to everyone *they* know? Better still, what if you had detailed
information about who they know so you can determine if they are the
right people to talk to? Now suddenly you have access to an endless
network of supporters — guides and experts who can answer your questions, give you feedback, connect you to more people, and help you accomplish things like planning your career before you even graduate from

college. This isn't a ficticious idea — this is a tool that actually exists. This tool is called LinkedIn.

LinkedIn is what helped Lylan Masterman secure the internship he needed to get ahead in his career — an internship that didn't even exist until he convinced an executive from across the country to create a job just for him. LinkedIn is what enabled Chris Stewart to get the word out about his interest in the company that ended up hiring him because his trusted contacts got his resume on the hiring manager's desk. LinkedIn is what Heather Pollock used to research the backgrounds of the interviewers who hired her for her first job out of graduate school. And finally, if it wasn't for LinkedIn, Joseph O'Brien wouldn't have landed his dream private equity internship in Australia, an opportunity made possible via an introduction by a grad school colleague who had the inside connection.

LinkedIn's membership is growing by the millions. In fact, one million people join LinkedIn about every 22 days. It may not be the largest *social network* (it's actually the fourth largest behind Facebook, Twitter, and YouTube), but it is the largest *business network*. As of fall 2010, it represents over 75 million professionals in over 200 countries and territories around the globe, and is growing by one person a second. As you read this, dozens of people are signing onto LinkedIn. But despite these jaw-dropping statistics, perhaps what's most important is not *how many* people are on LinkedIn, but *what type* of people.

LinkedIn's membership is what *Nielson Online* is calling "The world's largest audience of affluent, influential professionals." Not only is the LinkedIn population highly educated (over 80 percent have bachelor or graduate degrees), but it's also wealthy and successful. The average household income of the LinkedIn user is about $108,000 per year, and over 20 percent of LinkedIn users are senior level executives and managers. What's more, over 60 percent are either decision makers in their companies or have direct influence over key decisions related to product or service purchases. At this point, it's apparent that LinkedIn has an older audience compared to sites like Facebook and MySpace (although Facebook's audience is growing larger and older as we speak). As of summer 2009, the average LinkedIn user was 43 years of age.

Furthermore, we found that of the more than 75 million individuals with profiles on LinkedIn, only a mere 3 million or so are students. It comes as no surprise that most LinkedIn users are experienced working professionals. We're not suggesting that college students should be growing up faster or entering the workforce at an earlier age. What we *are* suggesting is that the membership gap between the experienced and aspiring professional be explored. We want to challenge you to view LinkedIn as an opportunity to reach the individuals who will play important roles in your development as a working professional, leader, or entrepreneur.

## Get an Edge on the Competition

About six months before graduating from Haverford College, Nick Farina was starting to get anxious about the job search. He did the usual thing — sent out a bunch of resumes and applied for jobs online — but nothing really happened. The first interview he got was because of a personal connection. He started to realize that if he was going to be successful in his job search, and in business, it was going to be because of his relationships. Fortunately for Nick, he was able to realize this sooner rather than later. As a result, he established dozens of connections with people who were ready, willing, and able to provide the support he needed upon graduation. He was eons ahead of his classmates.

As we write this book, the economy is slowly emerging from the worst recession since The Great Depression of nearly a century ago. You've probably already realized, it's going to take time for companies to begin hiring full-force again. What does this mean for you? According to the *2009 – 2010 Recruiting Report* (courtesy of Michigan State University), students seeking employment will continue to face fierce competition. Hiring levels per company are at the lowest levels in several decades, and we can't anticipate that there will be a job for every graduate in the next few years.

The good news is, as at any time in history, the patient and persistent will be the ones who find success. To open doors, you'll need to hone your skills, focus on your strengths, and create solid professional connections. The best way to battle through these rough times will be to get an edge on the competition. We believe the best way to get started is on LinkedIn, building your career support network while you're still in school, just as Nick Farina did.

## Transition from Social to Professional Networking

We've been talking about online networking for years, but what does it really mean? Networking online means using resources on the Internet to help you connect with people; it's just like networking offline. You can engage in online networking to look for a job, get more out of your work activities, or simply keep up with friends. Online networking is more than just using LinkedIn to make contacts; once you've established a LinkedIn profile, you should consider writing a blog, creating videos on YouTube, participating in niche online communities, tweeting on Twitter, or using a number of other resources to find, connect, and interact with people.

A social networking site is a large, web-based business that allows you to socialize and communicate with other like-minded individuals. Some networking sites, like Facebook, were started by university students for social purposes, and have since added business related features; others, like LinkedIn, began with a business networking focus and have since developed from there. LinkedIn and Facebook *do* have a lot in common. Besides the fact that they're both platforms for connecting people, they also require similar skill sets. In order to make the most of either network, users must learn to create and manage content, find and add the right connections, and interact with people online.

Many of you already have the technical skills and know-how to establish and maintain a social network account. As a member of Facebook or MySpace, you've already realized the power and value of social networking. You've been able to find your friends, friends of friends, family members, previous co-workers, and acquaintances from high school. However, while you surely enjoy being able to connect with these individuals, you're probably aware of the sparse amount of professional information available on their personal profiles. The small amount that is displayed is all too often out of date or inaccurate. Even the savviest networker needs more than Facebook has to offer to build a meaningful professional network.

When you want to get a group of your friends together for a party or event, Facebook is a great place to start. LinkedIn, on the other hand, is a tool intended for professional networking. If you want to meet people of influence in your industry or find local professional events, LinkedIn should be your first stop.

Now, you may be asking yourself, "Why should I begin professional networking in college? What's the benefit of building relationships when I'm not even sure what I want to do yet?" Whether you're an undergraduate college sophomore or in the midst of graduate school, networking will allow you to meet the people who can help you see the path to that first internship or job. It will enable you to establish a support network of people who can point you in the right direction. What we're encouraging you to do is take the social networking skills you already have and apply them in a professional manner. And if there's any place that will acclimate you to the world of business and professionalism, it's LinkedIn.

## Realize What You Can Accomplish with LinkedIn

At the start of this chapter, we mentioned that Lylan, Chris, Heather, and Joseph were all able to use LinkedIn to secure jobs and internships. What's important to note, however, is that LinkedIn can benefit you in any stage of the career planning process or during any year of study. We realize that not everyone reading this book is in the same stage of their academic or professional career. If you're a freshman in college, you may be getting acclimated to your new environment and just getting to know your professors and fellow students. If you're a junior, you may be more focused on your involvement in organizations on campus or thinking about internships. With that said, you might have a different set of goals from one month to the next. Perhaps you're in the process of choosing your major. Or maybe you're looking for a mentor to give you guidance on your career direction.

What can you expect to accomplish with LinkedIn? By following the Net-worlding approach to LinkedIn, you can expect to experience success in a myriad of ways.

For Courtney Dean, recent graduate of the University of North Carolina, LinkedIn helped her connect with past and current colleagues, as well as keep a fresh resume online to better market herself to potential employers:

"I began using LinkedIn as my 'online presence' when I was first applying for internships and jobs in college and post-graduation, and now I use LinkedIn as a way to track and maintain my network. I am very active on social networking sites, but I use LinkedIn as the 'professional version' of social networking."

Amber Sharma, recent graduate of The Catholic School of America in Washington D.C., uses LinkedIn to get advice from experts she feels she wouldn't have access to on campus:

"With LinkedIn, students can find plenty of information on an industry that they are looking to get into as well as the skills and requirements sought in successful candidates; real examples of peoples' career paths; and, if bold enough to ask, answers directly from mainstream professionals — all in one place. Beyond that, it's just a great resource with which one can supplement his or her education."

And finally, there's Steven Silverman, recent graduate of the University of Michigan at Dearborn. While we're writing this book, Steven is progressing through the interview process with a company he discovered on LinkedIn. Now he's using it to look up his interviewers and learn about their backgrounds so he can make meaningful personal connections:

"I cannot give all the credit for securing an interview to LinkedIn. It really helps to find people at your target companies and send them messages, but it's the job seeker's responsibility to stay in touch by email and phone until that interview comes along and even after the interview process, whatever the result."

As you can see, everyone has such a unique experience using LinkedIn to make connections and uncover opportunities. These are just a few key examples of what LinkedIn enables you to do:

- Create a professional online presence to get noticed by key professionals
- Establish, build, and maintain your professional network
- Learn about the companies, occupations, and industries you're interested in
- Conduct your job search and prepare for meetings and interviews

Now that you know what LinkedIn is and how it can help you achieve your career goals, it's imperative that you understand a critical point about social networking. As Steven Silverman suggested, never should LinkedIn or any other social networking platform be given 100 percent credit for success. LinkedIn is a powerful tool, and like any other power-ful tool, it works best when we take the time and responsibility to learn how to use it well. Far from replacing human interaction and reciprocity, LinkedIn can become a means of expanding and strengthening these important interpersonal connections.

Now we will share with you our approach to networking and how it can be applied to LinkedIn so that you can start thinking about how you will build your career support network.

# The Networlding Approach to LinkedIn

# CHAPTER 2

# The Networlding Approach to LinkedIn

What is Networlding, you ask? Networlding is a transformative concept. It provides us with a fresh perspective of how to move forward in our lives and careers, a vision that is critical to keeping up with our rapidly changing environment. When Melissa and Jocelyn Carter-Miller wrote *Networlding* in 2000, they knew that our society was beginning to measure accomplishments with a new yardstick, one of social connections and social impact rather than one of simply pay and promotions. They also saw almost a decade before others that one day a powerful online world would rise up from the broken pieces of the dot-com bubble (1995 – 2000).

Networlding shows you how to make connections with people you respect and trust, connections that will help you develop existing skills, find new skills and open up the way to fun, exciting projects. It helps you get your career off to the the right start, providing direction and focus as you begin to explore your dreams and passions. And the best part — Networlding, as you will see, works hand-in-hand with your social networks.

You're probably already using Facebook and other social networking platforms to keep in touch with your friends and seek opportunities, but the lines between personal and professional have blurred. Family, friends, and colleagues all mingle on Facebook pages, Twitter, and other places online; deciding how to act can be tricky. For some this has resulted in problems (some things are personal and should stay that way), but by being pro-active and establishing a few guidelines, you can avoid some of the most common headaches of networking. We'll show you how.

Some networking philosophies are simply superficial; they advocate a go-go, never-stop mentality. You may meet someone at career fair one day, and the next not remember why his or her card is in your wallet. Networlding is different. It's about making more purposeful connections that are meaningful and offer potential for a lifetime of success, for you and for those with whom you network.

Take Rachel Ropp. The first interview she landed was directly through LinkedIn. She had been applying for jobs online and attending networking events with little results, but then she tried reaching out through LinkedIn to alumni members at companies she was interested in.

Through LinkedIn she sent out several messages asking for advice and perspective. Like Paul Revere, Rachel needed to get the word out to the right people so she could accomplish her goal. According to Rachel:

"Everyone was helpful and willing to speak with me, and the first interview I got was with an alumni who spoke with me and then had me interview for a position that didn't even exist yet."

Although that particular job opportunity fell through, Rachel continues to use LinkedIn for job searching *and* relationship building:

"Any person I speak with or email, I research online. LinkedIn is extremely helpful for that; I can find common schools, interests, and cities we've both lived in —the kinds of things that make great conversation topics during an interview. I can also tweak my resume before I send it to an HR person; if they have a background in say, library or information, I add-in my library volunteer experience, which I might not have done otherwise, and that tends to help my resume stand out more."

Rachel's approach closely resembles the process of Networlding. In Networlding we emphasize connecting with people through "points of commonality." To this end, Rachel started out by approaching alumni from her college. This is an excellent way to connect with people; the commonality builds connection, and connection builds trust. But this is just the tip of the iceberg. Thoughout this book we will show you what you can do with this initial connection.

What's important to understand now is, in order to make the most of our connections; we need to understand how to use these connections for *mutual gain.* If the gain is only one-sided, the relationship quickly becomes unsustainable. Never underestimate an individual's perception; it's not hard to tell when someone is using you. If your connection feels this way, your phone calls, emails, and other efforts will be unwelcome.

Networlding is an approach you can use to achieve your ambitious objectives, and, as you will see throughout this book, LinkedIn is the perfect tool to supplement that approach. A Networlding perspective facilitates the development of meaningful connections and opportunities that benefit you, your classmates, and your community. LinkedIn will help you find these connections faster and give you a platform to initiate relationships that will make a difference in your life and in your career.

Before we jump into how LinkedIn can help you build your career support network, let's take a closer look at what Networlding is, as compared to the traditional view of networking.

## The Difference Between Networlding and Networking

Certainly there is a passing resemblance between Networlding and networking — both revolve around the concept of forming relationships. But the resemblance ends there. Networlding requires clear intent, compatible values, reciprocal exchange and support, and mutually developed, mutually beneficial outcomes.

*Intent* is an important part of Networlding. We use intent to mean forming relationships and opportunities intentionally — being highly conscious about the underlying values, goals, and beliefs that drive you toward a specific relationship or opportunity. Your intent may be to get involved as a leader in a student organization or obtain an internship, but it is also to know what beliefs and values are important to you as you pursue these goals.

The intent in Networlding is thus multi-dimensional. In contrast, networking is one-dimensional, focused on achieving one's goals by making the right contacts. The multi-dimensionality of Networlding means that your goals are tied to your beliefs. Instead of merely having a single, superficial goal like landing a job or closing a sale, you're more concerned with creating relationships with people who have the same passions as you do.

Networlding is a purposeful process of collaboration that not only achieves mutual goals, but also leads to professional and personal fulfill-ment. In contrast, networking is an often haphazard process of making contacts to achieve short-term, one-sided goals. Networlding is oppor-tunity-expansive. Networking is opportunity-specific. In a Net*world* rela-tionship, a series of opportunities flow from the partnership; in a net*work* relationship, people come together to take advantage of a specific op-portunity at best.

It's important to understand that while networking can be a selfish activ-ity, Networlding isn't a completely selfless endeavor either. You enter into Networlding relationships recognizing that they involve a continu-ous exchange of information, ideas, opportunities, and support. Friends, classmates, colleagues, and associates who are attracted to this idea of exchange will help you achieve your goals as you help them achieve theirs. Figure 2.1 summarizes the basic differences between Networlding and traditional networking.

| Networking | Networlding |
|---|---|
| Goal-based | Value-based |
| Duplication of efforts | Leveraged learning |
| Temporary | Long-term commitment |
| Transactional | Relational |
| Haphazard process | Conscious, strategic process |
| Often one-sided | Mutually beneficial |
| Fragmented | Systematic |
| Often Materialistic | Holistic |
| Superficial | Intimate |
| Opportunity Specific | Opportunity Expansive |
| Two-dimensional | Multi-dimensional |

Figure 2.1 **Networking Versus Networlding**

**Case in Point: Networking Versus Networlding for Jobs in School**

We've outlined the disparities between Networlding and networking, but what does this mean for a student who is trying to make connections for that first internship or job? The distiction between these two concepts becomes even clearer when you consider the experiences of Roberto, a consummate networker, and those of Lylan, a Networlding maven.

Roberto Martinez, an MBA student concentrating on marketing, needed a summer internship to satisfy some requirements for his program. Unfortunately, he had waited until May before he started looking so he really needed to pick up the pace in order to get something lined up for the summer. The good thing was that Roberto was outgoing, personable, and easy to get along with. As the president of a student organization, he knew a lot of people on campus. He was known for his ability to influence others and get things done, especially under pressure.

He decided that he needed to send a mass email out to all of his contacts telling them he was looking for a marketing or sales internship. He also attended several campus job fairs, passing his resume off to every recruiter he came across. Finally, Roberto visited his career placement office to get contact information for alumni. He searched the list for people working in the companies and roles he was interested in, compiled their email addresses, and sent a mass email to this group introducing himself and asking if they knew of any openings.

Two weeks and three replies later, Roberto managed to secure an interview for a retail management internship. One of his friends and fellow students, Lylan, heard about the internship while networking with some executives, but he passed on it because it wasn't a good fit for his area of study. Roberto wasn't particularly interested in this internship either — he really wanted to work in the marketing department of a large firm or advertising agency. However, since he was short on time, he settled for the retail management position and was scheduled to start working in less than two weeks.

Now let's contrast Roberto's experiences with those of a Networlder.

Lylan Masterman, an MBA student at the same university as Roberto, was interested in becoming a venture capitalist. Lylan realized that venture capital was a lucrative, but very difficult field to get into. Wisely, he began researching the industry and building relationships during his first year as in the program. Like Roberto, Lylan was very extroverted and personable.

He had no problem making contacts. In fact, he was known for his keen ability to find a way to help others before he asked for anything in return.

During his first year of graduate school, Lylan served in leadership positions for a venture capital club and an entrepreneurship club, and also got involved in several other organizations. He started networking in various groups specific to his career and industry, and like Roberto, he searched the alumni from his school for professionals working in venture capital; however, unlike Roberto, he did so to build relationships with them, not just to accomplish short-term goals. Finally, he joined LinkedIn so that he could connect with these individuals and research their backgrounds and connections.

Months before summer hit, Lylan was in the process of researching people and companies on LinkedIn. In preparation for a phone call with a professional in New York, he looked at the man's profile and discovered several "points of commonality" including the man's school and former employer, and used this information to build rapport. By the end of the call, the man suggested that Lylan look into a firm in San Francisco for an internship. He offered to introduce Lylan to his contact there so they could explore the possibilities.

So what happened next? Lylan had his call with the firm in San Francisco and discovered that they didn't have an available internship. Despite this, the firm was so impressed with Lylan's passion, drive, skills, and experiences that they created a position just for him! What's more, Lylan made all these connections, from a man in New York to one in San Francisco, all from his place of residence in Chicago.

What's the point?

In the end, Roberto and Lylan were both able to get internships they needed to satisfy their MBA program requirements. But while Roberto was forced to settle for something irrelevant, Lylan landed an internship that would take him one step farther down his dream career path. By being aware, looking out for others, and utilizing LinkedIn, Lylan was able to do what Roberto could not.

# The Networlding Exchange Model: Seven Levels of Support

We refer to networking connections as weak or flimsy because they lack support. In networking, people are bound together because one person needs another to do a favor, whether it be create a sale or pass along a resume. One particular situation binds them together, and as soon as that situation disappears, there's nothing left holding the relationship together. Networlders, on the other hand, are connected by the various levels of support shown in the support exchange model. (See Figure 2.2)

This model illustrates the hierarchy of the development of relationships. As you read on, think about how you may have received each type of support from your family, friends, classmates, and professors.

- **Emotional support.** Our feelings about others serve as the foundation for our relationships. The focus of exchanging emotional support with another is to create rapport, a relationship of mutual trust and affinity.
- **Informational support.** Information is a combination of messages. Once initial rapport is built, we then feel comfortable to share information of value.
- **Knowledge support.** Here, we add the element of experience. By sharing our personal experiences and those of others we have heard about, we add additional value to our exchanges with others.
- **Promotional support.** As we continue to build rapport, we naturally share with others the strengths of those whom we value. We raise our Networlding partners' awareness of others, and in doing so we better position them for opportunities that arise.

- **Wisdom support.** Wisdom adds the elements of clarity, understanding, and spiritual awareness. Wisdom exchanges are filled with caring and compassion — a real desire to help others develop and achieve their life's purpose. Here, there is also active mentoring and coaching based upon the years of experience others have accumulated.
- **Transformational opportunities.** Ongoing Networlding exchanges evolve into transformational opportunities. These opportunities are the result of continuous emotional, informational, knowledge, promotional, and wisdom support exchanges. Opportunities can be leads, referrals, new jobs, or something else entirely – professional or personal. Networlding exchanges at this level generate more and better opportunities. This process allows Networlders to pick and choose from a wide variety of opportunities. It also allows Networlders to direct their opportunities according to their passions and life stage. For a twenty-year-old, an opportunity to study abroad in Europe would be wonderful, yet not as welcome an opportunity for someone, say, in his thirties with young children.
- **Community support.** This level of support results from a series of exchanges. There is community growth that occurs as each Networlding partner shares the benefits of various forms of support with others in his or her community. As Networlding exchanges impact a Networlder's life, they create a ripple effect into the lives of others.

### Result? Fulfillment.

A deep, personal sense of satisfaction comes from finding your purpose, and then using that purpose to fulfill your destiny and create your legacy. Throughout the Networlding process, Networlders receive fulfillment from exchanges that they are making a difference in the lives of others. Fulfillment is both internal (i.e. self-satisfaction) and external (i.e. larger salaries or new business opportunities).

Remember, fulfillment is not something that comes without effort. It is the result of concious dedication and commitment to the process of Networlding.

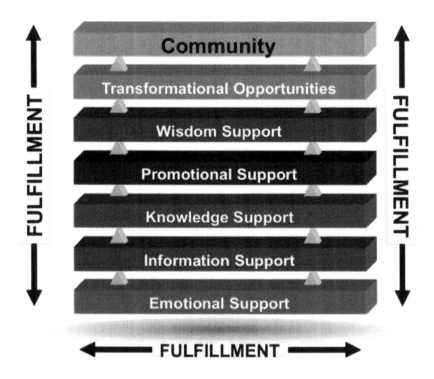

Figure 2.2 **Networlding Versus Networking**

At this point you may be wondering, if this model is based on an *exchange* of support, then what is there for me to offer my Networlding partners? How will I experience fulfillment at any level? Whether you're in your first year of college or you're just getting established in your career, you have much to offer the people in your network. You may not even realize it, but you've offered some of the different types of support already to your classmates and colleagues.

Perhaps you offered relationship advice to a classmate who at the same time was helping you with your homework (emotional support in exchange for knowledge support). Or maybe you used your Facebook skills to spread the word about your professor's research project (promotional support in exchange for wisdom support). As we begin to explain how LinkedIn can be used to make connections to build your career support network, start thinking about how you might provide support for your partners, either now or at some point in the near future. Later in the book, we will revisit the levels of support and explore more ways in which you can "pay it forward".

## Start Visualizing Your Career Support Network

Your Networld is a series of organic connections between you, people with resources, and new opportunities. Your Networld transforms and evolves with your intent and that of your Networld partners. Collectively, you give rise to mutually beneficial opportunities as you move toward your career goals. It's all about being cognizant of your interactions and striving for win-win relationships. Let's take a moment to wrap our minds around what a Networld looks like.

Imagine yourself at the center of a living, functioning organism. You are connected to many specialized cells that work together to accomplish the organism's various goals, like eating, breathing, and metabolizing. These cells work collectively according to what appears to be an invisible directive. They are efficient and productive, and each cell benefits from the actions undertaken by the others. As the organism grows, it changes form, learns new things, and gains new experiences. It adds, expels, and replaces cells. Finally, the organism combines with another organism to realize its greatest accomplishment: the creation of a new life. Sounds like freshmen year Biology class, doesn't it?

Similarly, in your Networld you are surrounded by cells — those in your primary, secondary, and tertiary circles. Like the specialized cells of an organism, each of these groups of people serve unique functions. Some have tremendous influence and are regular, active partners with you; others lend occasional but valuable support. This is a dynamic rather than static universe you've created.

If you can visualize yourself as part of this Networld — if this system strikes you as something that you want to create — then you're starting off on the right foot. Just shifting your thinking about the types of relationships you can develop will help you see the Networlding possibilities. If you have doubts about whether such a Networld is possible — especially if you're skeptical about your own ability to establish the right relationships — then consider this: you are closer to your future Networld partners and your career support network than you think, and LinkedIn can help you get there.

## Create Inner and Outer Circles

As we've already suggested, you'll need different circles of people surrounding you in your Networld. Relationships aren't all the same; Networlders quickly learn that if they organize their relationships according to type (frequency of contact, level of exchange, type of opportunities developed, and so on), they enjoy more productive relationships. Networkers, on the other hand, tend to have disorganized, undifferentiated relationships, and this prevents them from focusing their energy on the right people at the right time.

Organizing your Networld means dividing relationships into primary, secondary, and tertiary circles as illustrated in Figure 2.3. The primary circle is made up of people with whom you have frequent contact and support exchanges (i.e. At least once per month), and they're the ones most closely aligned with your goals and values. This primary group usually consists of ten or so influential individuals with whom you develop opportunities. In this circle relationships are proactive. People know

each other well and share beliefs and objectives, enabling them to anticipate the needs of others in the circle. There is a balance between asking
and giving.

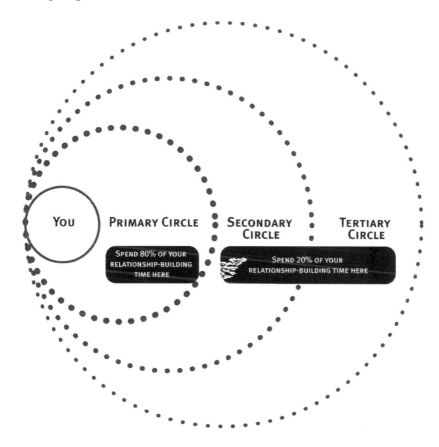

Figure 2.3 **Organizing Your Networld**

The interactions between people in the primary circle oftentimes lead to
additional relationships. Through the inner circle of your Networld, you
meet people who form the secondary and tertiary circles. Usually, someone in your primary circle refers you to an individual who then becomes
part of your outer circles. Because contact is less frequent, your secondary circle can be up to several times larger than your primary circle; main-
taining these relationships is important, but they shouldn't draw as much
attention or energy as your primary circle.

Secondary circles are valuable because they help you broaden your perspectives, expand your influence, and accumulate new insights. In most instances, secondary circles are more diverse than primary ones and can provide a greater range of ideas, information, and referrals. Tertiary circles are formed from the "overflow" of secondary circles. Tertiary circles consist of individuals you see least often but who can deliver — if infrequently — useful facts, ideas, and other types of support.

It is unrealistic to expect that you'll have equally strong bonds with every person in each circle. This is OK. Weak bonds may be fine, especially if your relationship with someone in a tertiary circle is built on an information exchange. As much as possible, however, you should strive to transition weak bonds into stronger ones. By doing so, you increase the chances of having successful, trusting Networlding relationships. Bonds built on trust produce the most valuable and sensitive insights, information, and opportunities. And as you will learn throughout your career, you are likely to invite someone to participate with you in a great business opportunity only if you trust and respect the person.

Because it's impossible to form strong bonds with everyone, you should concentrate on forming your strongest bonds with people in your primary circle; they're the ones with whom you have the most in common and the most contact. Besides your primary circle, also focus on creating exceptionally deep and meaningful relationships with the people we refer to as *influencers*. We'll dig deeper into this topic when we discuss how to expand your circles later in *Expand Your Career Support Network with LinkedIn*.

### Now that you understand what Networlding is, what now?

The actual practice of Networlding may seem intimidating. After all, it's one thing to attend high pressure networking events; it's something else entirely to establish circles and build mutually rewarding relationships.

We want to reassure you, however, that Networlding is something anyone can do. Although it requires a bit of thought and effort, there are ways to speed up the process when it comes to locating the right people and initiating the right relationships; this is where LinkedIn comes into play.

In the next chapter we will discuss the first step in jump-starting your career support network, and that is creating your professional online identity in the form of a LinkedIn profile.

**Networlding Tip:**

Throughout the book we will provide you with Networlding Tips that offer our best advice through many years of trial and error on making the best connections possible to ensure success. We also have many more of these tips on our Networlding Blog for up-to-the-minute new additions to LinkedIn.

# Crafting Your Identity on LinkedIn

# Crafting Your Identity on LinkedIn

The sooner you establish your professional online presence, the better off you'll be when it's time to build your network and look for career opportunities. Creating a professional online presence is a gradual process, so if you're in your first year of college or graduate school, you're certainly positioning yourself for success. Just ask Eric Kuhn, recent graduate of Hamilton College. He started building his profile and network during his junior year. When it was time to start looking for a job, he had already established good connections. In turn, these connections helped him land job interviews.

One of the most outstanding features of LinkedIn is the online resume platform it provides. Instead of just a single-standing Microsoft Word document, you now have a web-based resume that can be easily updated and shared with a global audience. Your LinkedIn profile allows you to display your professional experience, interests, capabilities, and notable achievements to a wide variety of professionals.

Your LinkedIn profile is specifically designed to attract the attention of important people who may be searching for you online — recruiters, potential employers, grad school admissions officers, and other individuals who could potentially become a part of your career support network. Think of your profile as a marketing document that showcases your skills and communicates the value you bring to the table.

Furthermore, your profile is your first impression, and therefore your best chance to differentiate yourself. Recruiters from some of the world's top companies are using LinkedIn as a primary sourcing tool, so having a sharp profile will increase your chances of being considered for future internships and job opportunities.

## Getting Started

Since most of you are familiar with social networking sites, we're not going to give you a step-by-step tutorial on how to sign up with the service. We're confident that you are savvy enough to Google your way to the LinkedIn home page, click **Join Now**, and complete the first step of the process by listing yourself as a student and filling out the required information.

The second step presents you with the option to see who you already know on LinkedIn and then upload your contacts. We highly recommend that you skip this step for now. Adding contacts is not what we need to focus on at the moment, so we'll move on. Once you confirm your email address and revisit your account, you're ready to click **Home** and see your current status.

What you see next is your home page. Immediately you'll notice a friend-ly "Welcome!" as well as the option to find people (see following screen shot). You may also see at the bottom of the page some classmates or colleagues suggested by LinkedIn. As cool as this seems, try not to get too distracted by this stuff; we'll cover what you need to know about adding connections in the next chapter.

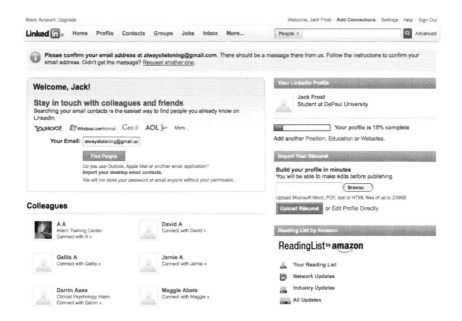

You may also notice that LinkedIn gives you the option to import your resume or CV. It may save you a little bit of time, but we don't particularly recommend it. See this as an opportunity for a clean slate. Chances are, whatever is on your resume may change drastically as you discover how you want to be perceived as a professional.

Now you're ready to start developing your identity on LinkedIn. Access your profile by clicking **Profile** at the top of the screen and then **Edit Profile**.

## Fill out the Basics

As you will see, LinkedIn fills in your name, headline, location, and education within what they call the "snapshot". They would like you to think of this portion as your interactive business card. But there are also a number of additional components, each making up a certain percentage of your profile completeness. Your page should look very much like the following screen shot; your profile will be 15 percent complete.

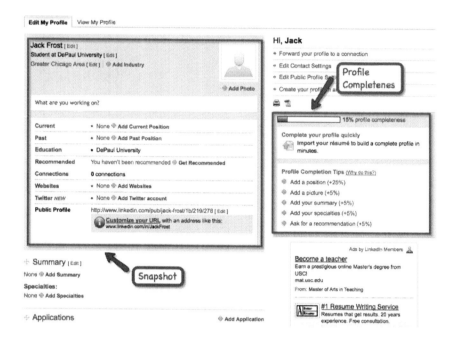

We'll go into more detail later about the significance of profile completeness. For now, let's focus on the basics — these are sections of your
profile that can be completed without extensive effort. Keep in mind that
you will need to insert the start date for your current position as well as
the start and stop dates for past positions and education.

The basics:
- Current Position
- Past Position
- Education
- Photo
- Additional Information

## Current Position

Now just because you signed up as a student doesn't mean that you
don't have options when it comes to filling out your current position. Are
you currently working for your university campus? Are you working part-
time at a restaurant or coffee shop? Are you in the midst of an internship

or co-op? Are you volunteering for a local community organization? Are you a member or officer of a professional organization, student group, fraternity or sorority? Any of these roles can be used to describe your current position, whether you're getting paid or volunteering. Make it known that you're doing something important. If nothing else, list your current position as "Full-time Student".

## Past Positions

Even if you're at the start of your college career, you should still be able to list some type of job or role you assumed prior to your current position. Ask yourself the same questions as we did for your current position. Again, this is your chance to showcase that you do have some type of experience, whether it be describing your summer jobs, internships, volunteer positions, or personal passions.

Check out John Exley's profile. This is a perfect example of a college student who leverages his involvement in campus organizations, and especially one in which he holds a leadership position.

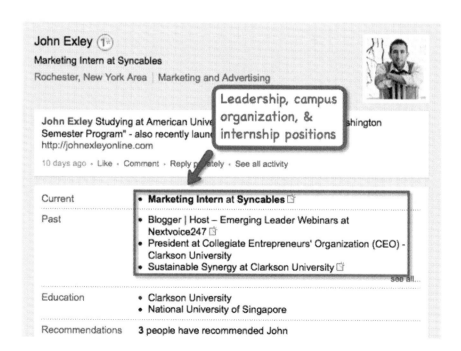

What about the position descriptions? When filling out your current and past positions, don't fret about the details of each position quite yet. We'll focus on this stuff later.

## Education

Although you already listed your current school or university, that doesn't mean you're done with this portion of the profile. Be sure to include information about all institutions you've attended, even your high school. This will help you later as you make decisions about who you'd like to connect to while building your network. Include your major and minor if you have one, as well as highlights from your activities and societies. It's also appropriate to include study abroad experience or summer programs. Don't shy away from showcasing your strong GPA and any honors or awards you may have received.

## Photo

Remember that LinkedIn is not Facebook or MySpace. If you choose to post a photograph — and we recommend that you do — select a professional high-quality headshot of you alone. Party photos, cartoon avatars, and cute pics of your kitty don't fit into the professional environment of LinkedIn. Your professional photo allows the people you've met and previously worked with to quickly identify you. Many people find it far easier to remember a face than a name — photos help bring that comfort to LinkedIn. Chris Stewart's profile below is a perfect example to follow.

**Chris Stewart** (1)
Senior Communicator at National Renewable Energy Laboratory
Greater Denver Area | Public Relations and Communications

Who should you make your profile photo visible to? LinkedIn gives you the option to make your picture visible to your connections, your network, or everyone. Your connections are the people you know directly; your network is comprised of people a degree or two away from you.

And everyone is, well, everyone. What you choose is your call. Jus
in mind that one of the main benefits of having a widely visible prc
being easily found by important people like potential employers.

## Additional Information

Don't let the title of this section fool you; it serves as much more than
just "additional information". Click **Edit** next to **Additional Information**
and you'll see where you can first add websites — an important way to
lend your profile more cachet.

For this portion, revisit what you listed for your current and past positions. Do any of these companies, organizations, or groups have a website? If so, click the **Add Websites** option on your profile; copy and paste
the web address and customize the name. For example, if you volunteer
for Habitat for Humanity, select **Other** in the drop-down menu and label
it so like we did below. Do you have a blog? If so, this is another great
opportunity to include the URL to your blog. Now when people visit your
profile, they will be able to click on these links and learn about your company, view your portfolio, or read your blog.

Next, list your personal and professional interests — anything that defines you, related to your career or not. Are you a champion cross-coun-
try skier? Maybe you're well-known for your abilities as a musician. This is
the place to communicate your talents as much as you feel comfortable.

Then, think about any groups or associations you are involved with. Perhaps you're a member of a student organization on campus or you recently joined a club for entrepreneurs. List these in the provided space.

Finally, polish off this section by touching on any awards or honors that may distinguish your work or education. Click on **See More** under each box to view more examples LinkedIn has provided for you. Adding this information not only rounds out your profile, but it also helps you turn up in search results when people search by keyword.

Now that you've filled out the basics, your profile completeness should be at least 60 percent as shown here.

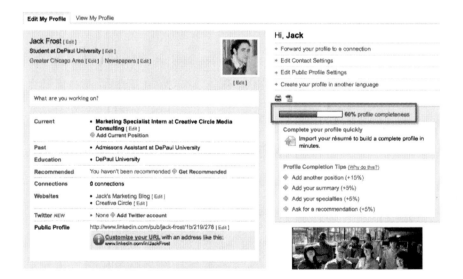

# Create Your Professional Brand

The next step in crafting your profile will take more time and effort. This is where you communicate your brand, summarize your goals and qualifications, and provide details about current and past positions. It's also a key component in optimizing your profile to appear in search engines like Google — one of the main ways potential employers could find you. We're calling this portion your professional brand.

Your Professional Brand:
• Headline
• Summary
• Specialties

## Headline

Your profile headline gives people a short, memorable way to understand who you are in a professional context. Think of the headline as the slogan for your professional brand. It can include information about your area of study, current work, or career ambitions. Examples of good headlines are "Aspiring Management Professional" or "Biotechnology Graduate Student" or "Recent Honors Grad Seeking Marketing Position". Take it to the next level by using unique language such as "Creative Marketing Strategist" or "Communications Catalyst". Check out the profiles of students and recent alums you admire for ideas and inspiration. Keep in mind that your headline can convey not only who you are, but who you aspire to be.

Under your headline, you may notice that your location is listed alongside your industry. Don't forget to enter an industry that best represents the type of work you're currently doing or which you aspire to do after school. For example, if you're majoring in Human Resources and have an interest in recruiting, you may choose "Staffing and Recruiting" as your industry. Don't worry if it doesn't fit perfectly. You can always update it later.

## Summary

Also referred to as your executive summary, your profile summary is your chance to summarize your professional brand. It should resemble the first few paragraphs of your best-written cover letter — concise and confident. Remember to include relevant internships, volunteer work, and extracurriculars. We even encourage you to express your passions as they relate to your field of interest. Don't be afraid to exhibit a little personality and write in the first person. Present your summary statement in short blocks of text for easy reading. Bullet points are great too, especially when listing your key accomplishments.

## Specialties

This section is the place to include keywords and phrases that a recruiter or hiring manager might type into a search engine to find a person like you. Think about the types of knowledge, skills, and abilities you have. What are your key strengths and talents? Speak to a specific technical skill (e.g. Adobe Flash, Microsoft Access) or a general job function (e.g. Recruiting, Event Planning). The best place to find relevant keywords is in the job listings that appeal to you and the LinkedIn profiles of people who currently hold the kinds of positions you're interested in.

Here's an example of Katie Andrien's summary and specialties:

## Summary

Health and Vocation Coach - providing coaching in the areas of health/wellness, nutrition, physical training, career/vocational, and personal/life. Moving towards certification as a Professional Coach with the International Coaching Federation. Certified Crossfit Nutritional Consultant and Level 1 CrossFit Trainer.

Industrial Consultant with Vincent Associates Inc. Specializing in industrial design and analysis, both external and internal.

Known to many as a genuine people person. The face to face time is what is most critical. Strong interpersonal skills and evidenced ability in leading clients to concrete goals.

Interests include health and wellness coaching, health research, physical training and nutrition, the employment of health within business, the balance between life/health and work, career coaching, and personal/life coaching. This is the system we exist in - the more we understand it the better we can use it to our advantage.

Outside interests include health/wellness and fitness, music and the arts, tango dancing, fishing, cooking, and exploring new people and places. Running, biking and CrossFit is a favorite past time. Through these passions Katie founded the Chicago School Athletics Team - the first athletics program at The Chicago School of Professional Psychology.

## Specialties

Health/Life and Business/Career coaching
Physical training & Nutritional consulting
Health Research
Industrial Design

## Work History

Once you've completed the basics and the professional brand of your LinkedIn profile, you're now at least 80 percent complete. You should then take time to focus on the details of your professional experience. Your position descriptions should briefly explain what the company does and what your main responsibilities and accomplishments were. Use clear, succinct phrases here, and break them into digestible chunks so even on a quick scan your accomplishments shine through. While typically similar to what's on your resume, you should be sensitive to financial numbers, launch plans, and any other information your past or current employers might consider confidential. Here are some other do's and don'ts to filling out the details of your work history:

## Do:

- Take time to fill out your profile; you don't have to do everything at once. You can edit, add, delete, and change the settings on who sees what at any time.

- Include keywords to allow HR professionals to find you, even if you aren't actually looking for a job when you create your account.
- Take the time to correct grammar and spelling.
- Spend 10 – 15 hours fine-tuning your profile (over a period of days or weeks or even months — not in one setting).
- Communicate what you've done, what you do, and who you aspire to be.
- Treat your profile like it's your resume.

**Don't:**
- Include information you don't want potential employers to see.
- Misrepresent your work, skills, or experience.

However you build your professional brand, just remember that it should speak to who you are, what you've done, and how you are able to add value to an organization or industry. It should also represent who you aspire to be as a working professional. Why would someone want to choose you?

When Nick Farina started building his profile during college, he looked at some of his connections' profiles and put himself in the position of a hiring manager. He asked himself, "What intrigues me about these profiles? What shows creativity? Which profiles have personality?" The ones he liked most were interactive and often asked: "What can I do for you?" Some were very professional, yet some were humorous and engaging. He decided to pattern his profile after those that got his attention, and so should you.

**Differentiate Yourself**
When you create a resume, your goal is to grab the attention of the person who's viewing it. One way to do that is to arrange the most relevant and impressive information at the top of the document. In LinkedIn you can simply go to **Edit Profile** and drag your sections to the desired location.

As a student with little work experience, you may choose to feature education first to highlight your area of study and involvement in campus organizations. Or you may decide to move work experience to the top to showcase your recent accomplishments with your internship employer. Alternatively, you could be a little more creative and use a LinkedIn application like Slideshare to present some important facts about yourself. More details on showing off your work will be presented later.

## Complete Your Profile: Request Recommendations

So now that you've completed the basics and your professional brand, you may notice that your profile is still not complete by LinkedIn's standards. Why do we care about profile completeness? Remember, your LinkedIn profile is your online business card, your resume, and your letters of recommendation all in one. Having a 100 percent complete profile increases your chances of being noticed by those who will potentially serve as members of your career support network. You can't build connections if people don't know you exist or see what you have to offer. According to LinkedIn, users with complete profiles are 40 times more likely to receive opportunities.

If you've completed every component of your profile except recommendations, then you're probably at 85 percent. If you receive recommendations from three separate members of your network, you will then arrive at 100 percent profile completeness (each recommendation worth 5 percent each). Nothing builds credibility like third-party endorsements. The most impressive LinkedIn profiles have at least one recommendation associated with each position a person has had.

In our experience, it seems that recommendations are the most discouraging part of the profile. If you have little work experience, it may seem difficult to find people to endorse you. On the other hand, if you were creative with your current and past positions, you'll have provided yourself with more opportunities to receive recommendations. What about the organization in which you volunteer? How about the student group you're leading? Just because you might not have "official" job experience doesn't mean you can't get recommended for work performed or services delivered within an informal work group or volunteer organization.

Here are some examples of the types of people you might consider asking:
- Former supervisors, managers, or bosses
- Professional mentors or academic advisors
- Business leaders and executives
- People you've worked on projects with or provided services for
- Former work colleagues or collaborators
- Fellow volunteers for a non-profit or campus organization
- Classmates familiar with your work
- Fraternity and sorority members

## Before You Ask

It's completely appropriate to ask others to write you a recommendation, if they actually know you well enough to write one. It's not wise to ask people who don't know you well or can't speak to your work. We recommend you go by this rule of thumb: if you've worked with the person in some capacity and you think they have something good to say about your work, it's probably appropriate to request a recommendation.

## How to Request a Recommendation

Requesting recommendations on LinkedIn is a very simple, three-step process. When you select Recommendations from the drop down menu under **Profile** (on the main tool bar at the top of your page), you'll be directed to the recommendations section. Click on the **Request Recommendations** tab and you will see the following form:

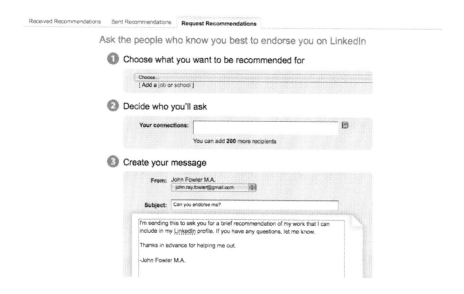

First, LinkedIn requires you to choose the position you want to be recommended for. Second, you are asked to list which connection(s) you'd like to ask for a recommendation. Third, the site prompts you to make your request.

This last message is the most important part of the process. No matter who it is you're asking, make sure to take the time to create a *custom* message. Even though LinkedIn provides you with a template, that doesn't mean you should use it. This is your opportunity to explain the basis and reasoning for your request; it's a chance for you to make the process of writing the recommendation as easy as possible. It also shows that you appreciate their time.

Here's an example:

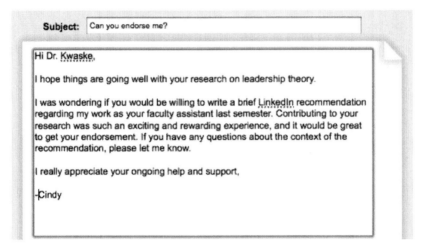

If you have trouble finding enough people to write recommendations for you, don't get discouraged. Many of you may be in the beginning stages of establishing and fostering relationships with the people who may be able to endorse you in the near future. As you progress through college or graduate school and gain more experience working with others in a professional context, there will be more opportunities for you to earn recommendations. As you work to establish and expand your career support network on LinkedIn, you'll connect with more and more people who may be able to speak on your behalf. Please see the Appendix for more examples of recommendation requests.

## Before You Start Connecting: Set Your Profile Settings

After you've crafted your profile, you're ready to move on, right? Not quite. Before you go any further, we highly recommend taking the time to personalize your account settings. The **Account and Settings** section allows you to customize how your information is displayed, how you want to be contacted, and your overall privacy preferences. We're not going to tell you what privacy settings to choose — we'll let you be the judge of that. But we would like to point out and make recommendations for another important item in this section. What we're referring to is your Public Profile URL or what is commonly referred to as your "vanity" URL.

## Set Yourself Up to be Found

When you click **Settings** at the top right corner of your page, you'll then be presented with information about your account status and links to various customizable settings. Let's first focus on the **Public Profile**. Click on **Public Profile** under **Profile Settings**. Here you can claim your vanity URL (such as http://www.linkedin.com/in/yourname) and control the publicly visible elements of your profile.

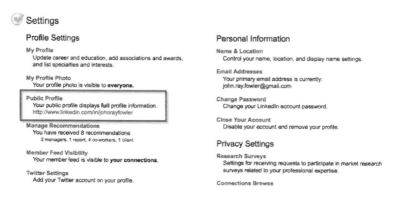

Creating a public profile URL allows you to be found on search engines like Google, Yahoo!, and Bing. Simply type in your custom URL and click **Set Address**. How do you decide what your vanity URL should be? In order to increase the chances of being found on the web, we suggest a custom URL consistent with how your identity is portrayed on other social networking sites. For example, if you list yourself as "Chris L. Allen" on Facebook or Twitter, then use "chrislallen" as your vanity URL. Later in the book we'll reveal some great tips that will help you use your vanity URL to expand your career support network.

Next, decide which parts of your profile are visible to the public. For example, if someone has come to your profile through a Google search, you can determine what your profile would look like to them (maybe you would only display your summary and current position, but hide past experience, education, websites, etc). Assuming you want to be found, first check **Full View** on the **Public Profile** and then check the various aspects you'd like people to see.

But wait! Not quite finished with your profile? Crafting your LinkedIn profile takes time, especially the components of your professional brand. If you're not sure you're ready for your profile to be viewable online, go to your **Public Profile** settings and make sure you select **None (off)** instead of **Full View**.

### Set Yourself Up to Receive Opportunities

Now go back to the main **Settings** page and click on the **Contact Settings** link under **Email Notifications**. This is where you control how you want to be contacted by others. Why is this worth mentioning? With LinkedIn, there's a professional protocol that dictates why someone can contact you. Consider that on your Facebook account you may choose "Friendship" under the "Looking For" option in order to avoid receiving messages from people looking for a new significant other. In the same way, LinkedIn has created an etiquette system for business communications.

For the type of messages you'd like to accept, you can choose to receive **Introductions** only or both **Introductions** and **Inmail**. For now, don't worry too much about this. We will cover these features later. But in terms of the kinds of opportunities you want to receive, we recommend you at least check **Career Opportunities** and **Requests to Connect**. This lets anyone who comes across your profile know that you're open to receiving inquiries about jobs and connections — both things you should be interested in as you start building your career support network and looking for jobs.

As you will see from the **Settings** section on LinkedIn, there are many other aspects of your account you can control. We highly recommend you take the time to consider some of these other settings at some point. On the other hand, if you have already chosen to present yourself on LinkedIn in a professional manner, then you might not have much negative information to worry about showing people anyways.

# Get Familiar With Your LinkedIn Home Page

We couldn't write a book for you about LinkedIn without talking about the home page. It's what LinkedIn calls "the dashboard to your professional world". For now, we'll just be covering the essentials so you can move to the next step of the Networlding approach to LinkedIn.

You can access your home page by clicking **Home**, the first link on the left of your top navigation tool bar.

Your LinkedIn home page provides you with an overview of what's going on in your network with Network Updates as well as the latest news, jobs, and answers. As you read this book and become more familiar with LinkedIn, you will learn to use your home page to:

- View your latest messages and get network updates from colleagues and connections
- Read the latest news about your company, competitors, and industry and discuss it with colleagues
- Browse the latest jobs, questions, and answers that match your interests

### Your Inbox

The first portion of your home page we'd like to cover is a simple, but key component — your inbox. **The Inbox** is the control panel for all of your LinkedIn interactions, including messages, introductions, and requests to connect or write recommendations.

Like any email system you've used, clicking on the subject takes you to your inbox to review and address the message. Alternatively, you can simply hover over the take action button to the right of your message to immediately reply or archive it. At the bottom of the inbox, Linkedin also lists the number of pending action items categorized by message type such as **Invitations** and **InMails**. Finally, take a short cut to your inbox by hovering over **Inbox** on the top navigation bar. This allows you to quickly get to your received, sent, and archived messages or compose a new message. You get the drill.

### Additional Modules

As you become more familiar with LinkedIn, you will discover a wide array of features and applications that can be used to enhance your profile, build your career support network, and search for jobs. You may join an industry-related group or download the SlideShare application. When you do this, new modules may appear on your home page. After a while, you may notice your home page has become cluttered or overwhelming. Not to worry, by clicking the blue title bar of the modules on the right hand side, you can customize the types and amount of information displayed.

If you want more information of a particular type, just add another module of that type via the **Add a Module** link at the bottom of the column. You can also drag and drop the modules to reposition them. When you see something interesting in one of these modules, you can click the link to take you directly to that content.

Throughout the rest of the book, keep your eyes peeled for "Home Page Tips". We'll refer to different aspects of your home page, including modules, that will help you stay in touch with your career support network.

### Ready to Jump-start Your Network?

The purpose of this chapter was to help you get started on LinkedIn. At this point, you should have at least created a profile you feel comfortable displaying publicly. If this is the case, feel free to go to **Settings** and change your **Public Profile** from **None** to **Full View**. Now you're ready to start building your career support network!

# Establishing your Career Support Network with LinkedIn

# CHAPTER 4

# Establishing your Career Support Network with LinkedIn

Though you may not realize it, you currently possess a powerful and wide-ranging set of contacts. It may include your father who knows a manager of a company interested in using you as a consultant. It may include a cousin whose best friend's father owns a company at which you'd be interested in working. It could even mean that a professor can provide you with a solid lead for a job. In other words, the connections exist, but you just haven't had the ability or technology to see and organize them. In this chapter, we will show you how to use LinkedIn to create this network. You will do this by following an easy process that allows you to quickly find and connect with people you already know.

The best way to establish your network is to identify the people you already know and then determine whether or not you want them to be a part of your career support network. Start by thinking of all the people you already interact with in the following categories:

- Family (immediate, extended, and distant relatives)
- Friends and friends of friends (acquaintances)
- Neighbors, roommates, and people in your dorm or residence hall
- Colleagues, co-workers, and team members
- Former bosses, supervisors, or managers
- Customers, clients, and vendors
- Professional service providers (accountant, lawyer, real estate agent)
- People you've met in community, volunteer, or professional organizations
- Career center staff, internship coordinators, and recruiters

Create a list of these people in a document or spreadsheet. That way, when you start looking to add connections on LinkedIn, you have all these *contacts* on hand. Now you just need to decide if they will make good *connections*.

## The Difference Between Contacts and Connections

Networkers have contacts; Networlders have connections. The difference lies in the depth of the relationships and how they're achieved. Networkers traditionally rely on the "law of averages": they attempt to get in touch with as many people as possible, hoping that a high quantity of interactions will produce a few good opportunities in the end. In contrast, Networlders spend more time up front building a relatively small number of relationships that will produce better and longer-lasting opportunities.

> **Networlding Tip:**
> **Identify Quality Connections**
>
> As you consider connecting with your existing contacts on LinkedIn, it's helpful to search for certain identifying traits — the qualities you would want in a Networlding partner. Power and influence don't always indicate a good connection. Similarly, individuals who are outside of the traditional networking circle may make excellent Networlding partners.

*Discernment* is the key to understanding what we mean by connections. If you're discerning, you look at prospective relationships perceptively. To form a meaningful connection, you must assess a potential relationship based on what will be exchanged. Will you and your partner provide each other with support? Will the relationship be strictly professional, or can you count on the other person to openly share feelings about a problem or opportunity? We've seen networkers who are pure ladder-climbers and have no meaningful relationships. Even if they succeed in the short-term, it's often empty success. These people aren't discerning in their relationships; they just form them without a second thought.

We list the following traits to help you recognize a good connection when you meet one, as well as to help you become familiar with the traits you need to develop in yourself.

- Supportive
- Continuous Communicators
- Reliable and Responsible
- Influential
- Knowledgeable
- Active Listener
- Empathetic
- Appreciative
- Connection-conscious

Now take this one step further. Think about all the people you've worked with in some capacity and experienced success with (not only in the business sense, but in school, in volunteer activities, and so on) who also had values that were compatible with yours. For instance, your project partner in school went above and beyond what you expected, making an effort to ensure that the work was evenly distributed and high caliber. You both received good grades in the class, and you felt you had a bond of mutual respect and accountability. This individual would fit the ideal profile of someone you'd like to have in your network.

In the same manner, when you start building your career support network, you need to decide which people among your contacts could be meaningful connections. Part of the discernment process is opening your mind to different relationship possibilities. Networkers tend to think narrowly: "Since I'm in the Electrical Engineering program at my school, I need to form relationships with experienced electrical engineers and engineering executives." Networlders embrace a world of relationship possibilities — from next-door neighbors in their dorms, to members in their organizations, to co-workers at their jobs. Once you open up your mind to these possibilities, you increase your odds of finding the people with whom you will establish powerful connections.

## Three Easy Steps to Jump-starting Your Career Support Network with LinkedIn

Now let's jump to LinkedIn to locate these people and consider connecting with them. Once you click the green **Add Connections** link at the top of the page, you're ready to jump-start your career support network in just three easy steps.

### Step 1: See Who You Already Know on LinkedIn

The first step in building your network is to "import" your address book and add those trusted connections who are already on LinkedIn. After selecting your webmail service (Windows Live Hotmail, Gmail, Yahoo!, AOL, or Other), LinkedIn will list all those contacts who you are NOT connected to on LinkedIn. You may notice that some of these people have **in** next to their name — this indicates that the person is matched with a profile on LinkedIn (see the following screen shot). Anyone without the symbol is either not on LinkedIn, or they are listed under a different email address. As a bonus, LinkedIn will also update contact information for you.

## Invite 286 Contacts to Connect

You have **286** contacts that can be invited and **139** are already using LinkedIn. Select which contacts you wish to in

**Send Invitations** or Cancel

At this point, you can look at each person listed and decide whether or not you'd like to connect with them. Keep in mind that just because they show up doesn't mean you know them well. Any person you've ever emailed using your webmail service may show up on this list, so you might want to use some discernment before you start sending invitations. Whatever you do, don't select all the names and have LinkedIn send invitations to the matches it finds. This robs you of the opportunity to make sure the people are ones you want to connect with and of the opportunity to personalize your invitation.

What about Outlook? In the event you use Microsoft Outlook, you can install the LinkedIn toolbar to Outlook and, with a click of a button, it will search your address book and your emailed messages for people on LinkedIn whom you could send an invitation. The latest version of the Outlook Toolbar can be downloaded by clicking on **Tools** at the bottom of the LinkedIn home page. If you use Act!, Palm Desktop, or the Mac

OS X Address Book, or most other contact managers or email applications, click the option for import your desktop email contacts. Browse for the file containing your contacts and upload it.

**Step 2: Send Invites Manually to Non-members**

Another way to build your network is to invite people who are not yet members of LinkedIn. If you are unable to find someone on LinkedIn and would like to try adding them to your network, simply enter their email address (like we did below) to invite and connect.

Don't get discouraged if you send someone an invitation to join LinkedIn and they never do so. As we know, not everyone uses the same social networking tools, and that's OK. They may respond to you by saying "What is this LinkedIn invitation you sent me?" or "I'm not sure if I want to join this network yet." This is a great opportunity for you to share the reasons you joined LinkedIn and the ways it will help you (and them) build a career support network.

**Step 3: Reconnect with Former Classmates and Former Colleagues**

Within the **Add Connections** section, you may notice the names of colleagues and classmates. This is the perfect opportunity for you to grow your network, and fast. For any of the current or past positions you included on your profile, LinkedIn populates all new and existing members of these networks. Just select the company or organization and search for people you know. The same goes for any of the academic institutions you have or are currently attending. After selecting a school, you can search for classmates by years attended or graduation year.

## Classmates / Search Results

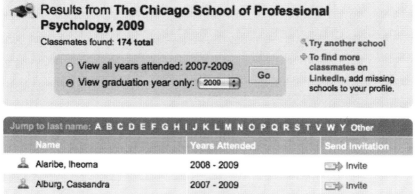

Hopefully this three-step process has allowed you to find some existing contacts and send them invitations. But, most likely, there's a significant number of contacts you were unable to find. Not to worry — LinkedIn has a powerful search engine that will not only help you find the remainder of your existing contacts, but will also enable you to conduct targeted searches for new connections. We'll cover this feature in an upcoming section.

Once you've found and connected with the people you already know, it's time to start thinking about who has the ability help you accomplish your goals within the next few years. Not that your existing contacts aren't valuable, but it's important to start thinking about with whom you'd like to foster more meaningful relationships. Also, start thinking about which of these people might serve as members of your primary circle. Who has the potential to exchange support and interact on a regular basis?

## Networlding Tip:
### Networlding Smarter, Not Harder — Focus on Your Primary Circle

In Chapter 2 we had you visualize your Networld in terms of primary, secondary, and tertiary circles. Again, your primary circle consists of people with whom you have the strongest bonds and most frequent interactions. Focusing more of your time and energy on these relationships yields additional connections and fruitful opportunities. Here are some steps you can follow to ensure your primary circle is well maintained:

- Initiate contact (by phone, email, or LinkedIn) with at least three people you consider prime candidates for your primary circle and who you've determined to be influencers.
- If the response is positive, schedule a meeting for coffee or lunch.
- If the meeting goes well, schedule additional meetings to exchange ideas, information, feelings, and opportunities.
- Tap into your partner's hidden connections (using LinkedIn).
- Continuously assess the three relationships to determine if they meet the criteria established for both Networlders and influencers.
- Repeat these steps whenever possible to add to your primary circle and to replace any individual who no longer belongs in that circle, but try not to exceed ten members.

**Networlding Tip:**

The Law of Reciprocation: Exchangers and Takers

Networlding is not about giving alone or taking alone. It's about exchanging. An *exchanger* is a person who understands the dynamic cycle of giving and receiving. Networlders have an eagerness to continuously exchange leads, information, and ideas. This understanding is critical to success.

Before connecting with people on Linkedin, think about whether that person is a taker or an exchanger. Use the following points as your guide:

| EXCHANGERS | TAKERS |
|---|---|
| **Exchangers** ask questions that demonstrate a concern for your issues and needs. | **Takers** ask questions that are focused on meeting their own needs. |
| **Exchangers** attempt to make sure that there is an equal exchange of information, leads, and so on. | **Takers** always ask for business or jobs. |
| **Exchangers** call you as much as you call them; they make an effort to stay in touch. | **Takers** only call when they need something. |
| **Exchangers** provide assistance without ever talking about how much they're doing for you or how much effort they're putting into it. | **Takers** frequently complain that your project is taking too much time and say they hope you'll be able to reciprocate when they need you. |

## Understand the Invitation to Connect

Unlike most social networking sites, LinkedIn promotes professional and trustful relationships. Connecting with someone on LinkedIn is not necessarily the same as adding someone as a friend on Facebook or MySpace; it implies that you know them well.

Before you start connecting, it's critical to first understand how you invite people into your network. At any point you come across someone you want to connect with, you will navigate to their profile and click **Add (person's name) to your network**. LinkedIn first asks you how you know the person. If they are (or were) a colleague, classmate, business partner or friend, you can send your request without entering their email address. However, in the event that you have no previous association with the person (the **other** option), LinkedIn requires you to have their email address.

But why can't you just classify them as a friend? Well, you can. We just recommend that you think twice about using this option, especially if it's not someone who knows you well. Oh, and what about the **I don't know (person's name)** option? This is sort of a trick question. Going this route will not allow you to send an invitation. Why? LinkedIn tries to protect everyone from spamming and strangers. Don't worry, we should be thankful to LinkedIn for this.

Now we'd like to draw your attention to the bottom of the invitation. This is where LinkedIn gives you the option to include a personal note (see the following screen shot). Although it's labeled optional, we highly advise that you avoid sending the "I'd like to add you to my professional network on LinkedIn" message unless it's part of a longer note. Think of it from their perspective. How would you feel if you received this note from a classmate you haven't seen since high school? We think you should make an effort to craft a personal message for the same reasons we suggested you customize your recommendation requests. What if you were at a party and someone approached you and said "I'd like to add you to my professional network of contacts?" You would probably think, "Really? Did that just happen? Who is this person? Why should I care?"

But what if they said instead, "A bunch of my friends at school told me about the amazing presentation you made about digital technologies. I'd like to grab lunch with you sometime to learn a little more about your work." Wouldn't that be more desirable? In the Appendix we have included some examples of personalized invitations just to get you thinking on how to approach this part of the process.

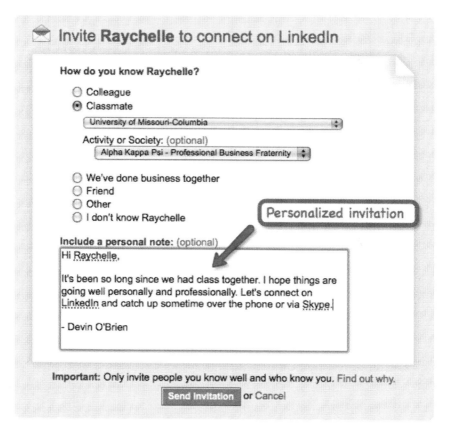

## Handling Incoming Requests

When someone asks you to join their network and you're not sure you want to accept, don't have an anxiety attack. Just take a moment and reflect on your networking values and preferences for connecting. First and foremost ask yourself, "How well do I know this person, if at all? How do I feel about this person having access to my network? Is there potential to have a mutually beneficial relationship with them?"

If your gut tells you it's not a good idea to connect, then don't be afraid to deny the request. The best thing to do in this situation is to ignore or archive the invitation. And don't worry, doing this will not send them a message of any kind that you've decided not to add them. It won't say anything like "Are you kidding me? I couldn't stand you in grad school and I can't stand you now!"

## Find More of Your Existing Contacts on LinkedIn

At this point you should have been able to find and connect with some of your existing contacts on LinkedIn. By using our "Three Easy Steps," you might have located family members, friends, classmates, and coworkers. For those people you were not able to locate, we recommend compiling a written list or electronic document that includes all of your existing contacts that could result in additional connections on LinkedIn. Again, these are people you already know that have potential to be part of your career support network (e.g. professors, career center staff). How do you find them? The answer is simple: LinkedIn **People Search**.

### LinkedIn People Search

The right person, knowledge, and expertise you need is already on LinkedIn; now it's just a matter of learning how to use the site's search function so you can locate the potential networking partners you have on your list. In this section, we will introduce you to LinkedIn's search tool and show you how you can use it to locate more connections.

Take a look at your list of potential connections and pick the name of someone you'd like to connect with on LinkedIn. The easiest and quickest way to conduct your search for this person is to type their full name in the search engine at the top right corner of the page (make sure the **People** option is selected). As you can see in the following screen shot, we were able to easily find Barack Obama using this method. But in the event that you don't have the person's full name or you're not sure on the spelling, LinkedIn allows you to filter your search according to location, industry, company, school, groups, and even by degrees of connection. This section appears on the left side within the **Find People** tab. You can also click **Show More** to search based on the same criteria just mentioned (plus an option for job title), but LinkedIn allows you to enter it more quickly.

The fabulous thing about this feature is that you don't need to know the person's full name or have exact search terms. Just type in the relevant keywords and hit **Search**. For example, let's say you had a brief, but good conversation with a recruiter at a job fair on campus. You can't recall her full name or even her company because it was months ago, but you do remember being excited because she mentioned working out of Boston, which is where you would like to work after graduation. Not only that, she was also an alumna of your college. In this case, you can find her by typing her first name in the **People Search** engine and then filtering according to location and school.

If that doesn't work, you can also search according to job title. In this case you would check the box for **Keep filter selections** so that you still search according to location and school, but then you would click **Show more...** and add the title. Even though you might not know her exact title, you can use a little trial-and-error by entering a number of different titles. For a recruiter you might try searching "recruiter", "recruiting manager", "recruitment manager", or even something along the lines of "talent acquisition manager". More often than not, this is all the information you need to find someone on LinkedIn.

There is also an option for an **Advanced People Search**, which is arguably the most effective way to find professionals, especially those you'd like in your career support network. In the next chapter we'll explain how you can use this feature to find specific people who can help you achieve your career goals. Some of these individuals may become members of your primary circle and others may become secondary and teriary connections – whatever the case, they could be valuable members of your career support network.

### Just joined LinkedIn

COLLEAGUES
**Business Training Library**
**Enterprise Rent-a-Car**
**The Chicago School of Professional Psychology**
**Leo Burnett**
**JR Consulting**
**Enterprise Fleet Services**
**Monar Consulting**

CLASSMATES
**The Chicago School of Professional Psychology**
**University of Missouri-Columbia**
**Oakville Senior High**

### Homepage Tip:
**Find More Colleagues and Classmates who Just Joined LinkedIn**

Wondering which of your colleagues and classmates are on LinkedIn? The **Just Joined LinkedIn** section highlights new LinkedIn users who have worked or attended the companies and schools listed on your profile. Just click on these links, find the people you know, and invite them to connect. This is a great way to add more people to your career support network. If you don't see a company or school in the **Just Joined LinkedIn** section, make sure to add it to your profile.

# Expanding Your Career Support Network with LinkedIn

# CHAPTER 5

# Expanding Your Career Support Network with LinkedIn

Wouldn't it be great if we could create a career support network just from the people we already know? It would save us a significant amount of time and effort. Unfortunately, the people we know aren't always ideal connections. Their values don't necessarily match ours, or they lack the qualities essential for good Networlding partners. Don't forget that the whole point of Networlding is to establish and foster *new* relationships.

In the last chapter, we had you focus on jump-starting your network by connecting primarily with those people you already knew from the following categories:

- Family (immediate, extended, and distant relatives)
- Friends and friends of friends (acquaintances)
- Neighbors, roommates, and people in your dorm or residence hall
- Colleagues, co-workers, and team members
- Former bosses, supervisors, or managers
- Customers, clients, and vendors
- Professional service providers (accountant, lawyer, real estate agent)
- People you've met in community, volunteer, or professional organizations
- Career center staff, internship coordinators, and recruiters

Hopefully, you were able to connect with many of your existing contacts and begin using LinkedIn, in tandem with these relationships, to seek out new opportunities. However, while these people may serve as valuable members of your network, there is another important group of individuals we have yet to discuss. We refer to these people as *influencers*.

# Your Most Valuable Connections: Influencers

We define influence as the power to affect another person, group of people, or course of events. Although position and wealth certainly confer influence, we've found that good connections have *earned influence*; that is, they've achieved their power to influence based on a particular set of skills, knowledge, and accomplishments. In a Networld, influence is a mutual quality; both partners use their power to help each other accomplish important goals.

In our perspective, influence is not a passive or title-based concept. Just because someone is a CEO in your industry or has accumulated a great deal of wealth, doesn't mean he or she has influence. Influencers are doers, not observers. They will act on your behalf rather than just talk a good game. Someone who has made his fortune or achieved his title may once have been an influencer, but without ongoing action you can consider them retired.

It's very easy in our society to be impressed by titles, but there are influential people out there who don't hold prestigious titles. For example, an administrative assistant may be able to influence events through her innovative ideas and sound suggestions; she may be connected to other influencers through her job, family, or friends. People listen to what she has to say, and they trust her judgment. When she recommends other people and their ideas, her recommendations are acted upon.

### Behaviors and Traits that Characterize Influencers

Here are six behaviors manifested by influential Networlders. These behaviors may not be what first comes to mind when you think of influential people. They are:

- Willingness to give
- Community involvement
- Awareness of others' needs and interests

- Dependability
- Persistence
- Conscienciousness

However, influencers aren't easily identified by their behaviors. After all, there are many giving, community-minded, dependable people in the world who have very little influence; they simply don't make an impact, despite all their good qualities. Impact comes from a few attributes, and influencers have at least one of them without question. Here are the types of qualities or "assets" you should be looking for in the people you interact with:

- Broad base of knowledge
- Large perspective
- Difference-makers
- Active in organizations
- Skilled communicators

**Industry-specific Influencers**

Industry-specific influencers have the same qualities that regular influencers have, but they happen to be particularly influential in the industry in which they work and in which you are interested in working. Here are some examples:

- Corporate-level executives (i.e. CEO, VP)
- Mid-level managers or directors
- Key organizational or community decision makers
- Experienced working professionals
- Experts and knowledge leaders

It is very likely that you don't have a lot of industry-specific influencers in your career support network right now, and that's completely expected. Your next step in building your network should be targeting these experienced professionals, especially within your field of interest. These are the people who could be integral members of your career support network — potential mentors or future employers.

> **Networlding Tip:** Keep Track of Your Networlding Relationships with LinkedIn
>
> In "The Networlding Approach to LinkedIn", we talked about forming primary, secondary, and tertiary circles. You will find that as your career support network grows in size, it's much more difficult to keep track of your connections and where they fit in your Networld.
>
> Try this: create and save a list of the names of the people you've designated for your primary circle. Go to **My Connections** (under **Contacts** on the LinkedIn tool bar) and tag this group using the tags feature. Create your own and call it "Primary Circle".
>
> Do the same for key people in your outer circles. You might decide to create a label called "Industry Influencers". Stay aware of what these people are doing. Though you don't have to maintain regular contact, you should occasionally communicate with them (we recommend once every few months). No matter what circle your connections belong to, your joint success will be based upon your ability to initiate relationships with them in which meaningful exchanges occur for both of you.

## Mentors: Your Guide to Career Success

Mentors have the potential to be the most important influencers in your career support network. Like other influencers, mentors can be company executives, industry experts, or even alumni from your school who have acquired experience in your field. If you've already reached a point where you feel confident about your choice of major, you may be ready for a mentor.

Finding a mentor is more important now than ever. As we discussed earlier, the job market will continue to be competitive, and one of the best ways to stand out from the crowd is to seek out advice from someone who is doing exactly what you are aspiring to do with your career.

Experts have seen a dramatic shift in the way mentoring relationships are created and sustained. The traditional perspective assumes that the purpose of mentoring is for an older, more experienced professional to provide knowledge, guidance, and support for a much younger, inexperienced person. It also suggests that the mentor should be the one to initiate and control the relationship.

Today, successful mentoring relationships are characterized by people who simply share the same professional interests and ambitions, regardless of the age difference. Research has actually shown that some mentors benefit from the relationship as much or even more than their proteges. And instead of mentors taking charge, it is now more common and expected that the mentee initiate and manage the relationship.

What does this mean for you? As students and aspiring professionals, it is up to you to take ownership of your career and, therefore, take the time to find and connect with a mentor who can help you pursue your career. And although you may feel like you have nothing to offer your mentor, you actually have much to contribute — fresh ideas and approaches, strong technological skills, and innovative thinking. Remember the seven levels of support? Without even realizing it, you could have a significant impact on your mentor.

While writing this book, John fostered a mentoring relationship with Bob Dean, a senior level executive with over 25 years of experience in his field. Bob offered him guidance by sharing his knowledge and identifying areas where John could improve his work. He also exposed John to his network of professional connections, introducing him to key industry influencers (notice the number of connections on Bob's profile). To Bob's surprise, John reciprocated by offering informational, knowledge, and promotional support. He shared fresh ideas and best practices he learned from graduate school and his recent consulting projects. He even jumped in and volunteered to help Bob find customers for his business.

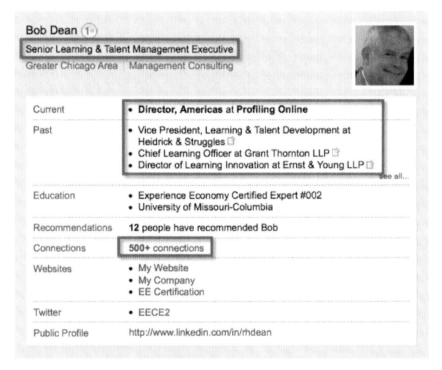

## Summary

Bob Dean has over 25 years experience focused on strategy and innovation in learning and talent development. Bob has served as a Chief Learning Officer and a global learning leader for the past eight years and now serves as a trusted advisor to clients focused on talent management strategy and solutions. Bob combines business experience with a passion for designing, developing, and delivering breakthrough learning and talent development experiences and driving business impact.

So you may be wondering how John found his mentor. John met Bob through Eddie, whom he in turn met through Melissa. And if you remember the story of how this book came to be, John met Melissa through LinkedIn; and without LinkedIn, John would not have known that his mentor was only three degrees away.

How can you go about finding a mentor? Consider the following steps you can take to establish a good mentoring relationship:

1. Make it a priority to find mentors in your field you genuinely admire.
2. Find those who have a presence on LinkedIn. (Note: target even further by finding people in your area, if possible. This way you can meet in person, which will be even more connective)
3. Take the time to examine their profile and, hopefully, they have a blog where you can get a good idea of what matters most to them and where you have something in common (points of commonality) — that's what they value and that's where you start connecting.
4. Write a short note referencing your points of commonality and requesting a short meeting to talk further.
5. During the meeting make sure you keep track of the time so that you keep within your original time request.
6. At the end of the meeting, ask if they would be open to a couple of mentoring sessions.
7. If they agree to mentoring, schedule one or two more sessions before you end the meeting.

If you don't find a mentor right away, don't get frustrated. Influential people may seem to be out of reach, especially if you're in your first years of college. With LinkedIn, however, they are well within reach. In this chapter we're going to show you how and where to find influencers on LinkedIn through **Groups**, **Answers**, and **Introductions**.

**Networlding Tip:**

**Learn About Influencers Online and Off**

When you consider the qualities of influencers, it's important that you have a general idea of how you might identify them and even find a place or situation where you'd be likely to encounter them. Influencers are not a rare species, in fact, they're everywhere around you. They are leading organizations, publishing articles or blogs, organizing your community, becoming leaders in charities, and speaking at events. The steps you take to find influencers will be guided in large part by what you wish to accomplish and who you feel would make a great member of your career support network.

It may seem like a no-brainer, but the first step you can take to learn about influencers is to...read! This might not be an essential step for some of you, but it's astonishing how many viable influencers you can uncover just by reading a variety of publications on a regular basis. Trade magazines, business journals, personal websites, blogs, and forums are all great places to seek out industry leaders. You would be surprised by the insights you will get by visiting a leader's blog. Often you will see that they don't actually have a lot of followers and that because you are more internet savvy than most, you will actually have a better pathway to connect. Use the edge you have with computer and social media skills to gain better connections.

One of the best ways to meet new professionals in your industry is to get involved in groups. Professional, volunteer, and campus organizations are all great environments for meeting people in your field of interest. For nearly every one of these organizations, there's a LinkedIn group you can join to connect and engage with these people.

# Engage and Connect with Influencers: LinkedIn Groups

When Chris Stewart enrolled in graduate school at the University of Denver, he knew that tapping into his university's alumni network was one of the best ways to jump-start his networking efforts. He visited the school's career center, asking them if they had a database or directory of the school's alumni, expecting them to email him a spreadsheet or a link to a database. Instead, the person in the career center referred him to the most accurate and up-to-date resource available, LinkedIn.

One of the best ways to meet new professionals in your industry is to get involved in groups. Professional, volunteer, and campus organizations are all great environments for meeting people in your field of interest. For nearly every one of these organizations, there's a LinkedIn group you can join to connect and engage with these people.

Over the past few years, there has been an explosion of groups on LinkedIn, and the site itself has shifted its focus to emphasize groups. From job support groups to professional associations, groups are now the hub of activity on the site.

LinkedIn allows you to join up to 50 different groups. Of course, if you are just beginning to explore groups, our suggestion is that you start by developing your presence on just a few groups; try an alumni group, a professional group, and a volunteer or extracurricular group. As a member, you can comment on discussions, find exclusive job listings, and meet people who share common interests. Even groups that don't have direct ties to your industry can be beneficial as long as you are able to create meaningful relationships there. For example, Nick Farina still keeps in touch with individuals from a frequent flyers group he joined in his early days on LinkedIn. The common interest was enough to spark discussions that lead to real bonds.

How do you find and join groups? It's simple, really. Click on **Groups** on the main toolbar and search the **Groups Directory**.

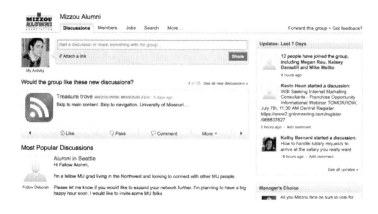

Most groups will require that you request to join. Owners choose this as a setting when they create the group. However, while you can't get a full picture of what the group is like, you do get a sneak peak at who in your network is also in the group. If the group turns out to not be quite what you expected, you can always leave at any time.

Once you've joined a group, it will appear on your left side navigation bar under **Groups**. Click on the **My Groups** link to view all of your groups. This page gives you a quick overview of all of your groups and allows you to access the home pages for each of them. Now that you understand the benefits of groups, and the process for finding and joining them, it's time to focus on what we believe is the most important group feature: the **Discussions Forum**.

### The Discussions Forum

The **Discussions Forum** is where the magic happens within groups. As we mentioned earlier, this is your chance to engage with industry experts, potential employers, possible mentors, and experienced professionals who can help you accomplish your career goals. The owner of the group may set some ground rules or standards for discussion, but most of the time, this is a place where people post announcements about upcoming events, requests for expertise, and even job opportunities. Just keep your eye out for posts from the owner about any rules and do your best to respect and abide by them.

Within **Discussions** you can start your own discussion, contribute to an existing discussion, or simply follow a discussion. The key to starting a discussion is choosing a relevant topic that will invite others to add comments. Once you initiate a discussion, you should make a point to engage with others and respond to their posts. If you choose to enter an existing discussion, it's wise to stay on topic and make contributions that not only add value to the discussion, but challenge others to think critically. Some people choose to follow a discussion by just reading and learning about a topic of interest without contributing to the conversation. This is completely fine. There can be much to learn from discussions, but just remember that the key to creating opportunities is *interacting* with others.

**Networlding Tip:** Keep Your Audience in Mind

As you become more familiar with LinkedIn and begin to use it on a regular basis, you may discover that everyone uses it differently, especially when it comes to networking and communication. Our advice is to take your interactions off LinkedIn as soon as you can. Using it as a primary communication channel may work with some people, but not others. People develop preferences both for channels of communication and for forums within these channels. One person may love meeting for lunch, another meeting in a virtual chat room such as Skype. Your job is to figure out where you'll both feel comfortable.

Often, the key to knowing your audience is seeking to understand the generational differences in communication styles and preferences. Some experts believe that generational differences in communication style will actually benefit the business world. Despite noticeable differences in the way different generations work and communicate, there is evidence that these differences in attitude may improve productivity in the workplace. So, how can we get to know and understand each other? Adjust your attitude, embrace your differences, learn from each other, and adapt accordingly.

**Leveraging Groups to Make Connections with Industry Influencers**

One of the biggest advantages of being a member of a LinkedIn group is that right off the bat, you have something in common with its members. Whether it's your school's alumni group or a professional association within your field, you are one step closer to creating a bond with influencers who might share your interests and passions. By interacting with people in the discussions forums, you create opportunities to relate to and connect with industry influencers.

When you're ready to connect to these influencers, the fact that you share the same group overrides the requirement to enter their email address. Even better, you're able to send them direct LinkedIn messages without having to get an introduction from one of your first-degree connections (we'll cover introductions later). Being in groups makes reaching influencers a much less daunting task.

Consider Henric Haldeborg, current student of Cleveland State University. During his mediation class, Henric's professor mentioned that he had created a LinkedIn group devoted to mediation and arbitration and that he would be happy to let any interested students join the group. So what did Henric do? Well, he joined the group and started participating in some of the group discussions. As he interacted with members of the group, he began to establish on-going relationships with them. It wasn't long before he landed an internship with potential to become a full-time, permanent position once he was done with school:

"What I am saying is, in your quest for that elusive foot in the door, you have to be where the right people are. Pick your groups and join in on the fun (or start some of your own). Show interest, initiative, and a willingness to learn. Before you know it, the right people will notice."

Joining discussions is one way to meet influential professionals. Creating your own discussion, however, is a better way — if you do it right. Lauren

McCabe of Northwestern University did exactly this. While on the hunt for a job, Lauren started a discussion in the form of an announcement, offering her services to any employer willing to take her on for a marketing project — for no pay. After posting the announcement in several of her groups (she custom tailored her message to each audience), she heard back from two individuals. One professional from a sustainable packaging company asked her to meet for an informational interview. The other contacted her from a company based out of Korea and was quite interested in making something work. Although she didn't get a job right away, she was able to use her Networlding skills to foster long-term relationships with these people. Months later, she was still in touch with these influ-

## Networlding Tip:
### Find Connections Through Volunteering

One of the best ways to build your career support network, especially with influencers, is through volunteering. Make an effort to volunteer for organizations you believe in. Volunteering is not only a great opportunity to make your values known, but also to meet influencers from all walks of life. We've found that some influencers put as much, if not more, energy into their volunteer efforts as their regular jobs. Many have made significant sums of money and are set for life; now they've turned their attention to matters that are more meaningful to them. And that's why volunteering presents an opportunity to make a connection that is more meaningful than simply a business relationship.

In volunteer work, simply be aware who's working with you on the project, activity, or effort. When you find an influencer, strike up a conversation about the work you are doing. Use that common purpose as a starting point for a relationship and see what develops. If there's some value-sharing and meaning behind your conversations, don't hesitate to connect with them on LinkedIn.

encers. Last we heard, she was in talks with the gentleman from Korea about a job opportunity in her city of residence!

### Search and Follow in Groups

There are a couple more key features within LinkedIn **Groups** that can help you target potential members of your career support network. The first is the **Members** page, which allows you to view all the members in your group (click on the **Members** tab). You can either scroll through the entire list or enter search terms by name, company, and other keywords. This is a great way to find people who can help you locate and communicate with influencers. Finding and targeting individuals will be explained further when we cover LinkedIn **People Search** in more detail.

The second part of **Groups** worth mentioning is **Following**. This feature provides an easy way to track contributions from your network and share your own activity across groups. **Following** allows you to filter for relevant, valuable contributions across all the groups you share on LinkedIn. For example, let's say you want to visit your university alumni group and catch up on the discussion you entered about how to pick a college major. Instead of fishing around for that discussion, you'll see that you are following it by looking at the right hand side of that group's page.

To get started, simply click on **Follow** next to any name in your group. You'll then be able to view contributions from that user on the **Following** tab in your **Groups** page. To see who's following you, scroll down to the **People Following Me** section.

### Take the Lead: Form Your Own Group

As a student, one way you can really stand out from the crowd is by creating your own group. Doing so will allow you to lead the group, giving you more control over the content and establishing youself as a leader. This action will help you build your professional presence as well as attract industry influencers who might just end up becoming members.

If you choose to create your own group, the following steps will help you avoid some of the pitfalls we have seen other groups encounter:

1. **Decide the purpose or objective of the group.** Is the group's purpose to simply exchange information? Will it be to collaborate on projects? Without a clear purpose, the group will grow slowly, if at all. Express the group's purpose to its members and facilitate it as much as possible.

2. **Build a group around a similar target market.** Suppose you are considering creating a marketing group (public relations, account planning, interactive, advertising) or just a public relations group. By creating a group that is more targeted, the public relations group in this case, you increase the odds that what you and other members provide will be of value to everyone in the group.

3. **Make your standards clear and up front.** Check out the following screen shot for an example of the standards Melissa sets forth in her Networlding Group:

## Learn from the Experts: LinkedIn Answers

Now that we've covered ways that you can use LinkedIn **Groups** to create opportunities for connection, we'd like to introduce a very similar concept: LinkedIn **Answers**. Just as there are groups for discussions, there are groups for asking questions. Click on the **Answers** link on top of the page under **More...** and you'll discover another way to engage and connect with potential members of your career support network.

Before you start asking questions, we recommend that you first familiarize yourself with this feature by by looking at the types of questions people are asking and the responses they're getting. You can either look at the **New Questions from Your Network** or go to the **Answer Questions** tab to browse all open questions. If you'd like to see questions within a general category, choose one from the list on the right side of the page.

Once you get a feel for how it works, go to the **Ask a Question** tab and start thinking about what you'd like to ask. Is there a particular topic you're researching for a school project? Are you looking for new, better approaches to solving problems at your internship? Are you looking for advice on entering your industry of interest? Having a well thought out question is important, so don't be in a rush. If you click on the **See examples** link within the **Ask a Question** box, you'll find some useful information regarding good and bad questions. You can also get tips from the **What should I ask?** link on the right side of the page.

Once you've entered your question, you'll be presented the option to either share it with select connections or open it up to the public. Depending on how focused your question is and who you'd value feedback from, sharing with select connections may be appropriate. Just remember, the power of this feature, what truly differentiates **Answers** from **Groups**, is the potential to reach a wider variety of people around the world, giving you access to more diverse and valuable feedback, not to mention more answers overall.

Next, you'll want to provide some details about your question. If possible, provide additional context for your audience; this will help them provide more relevant, specific responses. Then, try to categorize your question as best you can so that people are able to quickly identify if it lies in their areas of expertise. You'll also need to decide if your question is geographically specific. Finally, if you're question is job-related, check the box for **job-seeking**; otherwise leave them all unchecked.

Here's an example of a well-written question and its additional details:

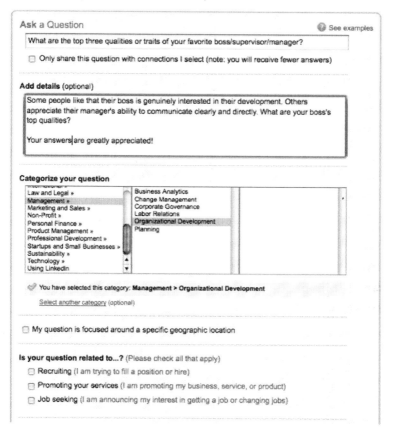

Once you've posted your question, LinkedIn will keep it open for seven days unless you decide to close it earlier. In either event, LinkedIn will ask you (the question asker) to select one as the best answer. The person who gave that answer will then have a star displayed on their profile, recognizing them as an expert on the subject, having given one (or more) best answers. In addition to actual recommendations, this is a great way to gain recognition in the field.

## Use Answers to Get Career Advice

Amber Sharma, recent graduate of The Catholic School of America, found **Answers** to be the most helpful feature on LinkedIn. How does she use it? She asks intelligent, targeted questions about her field of interest, and in return she gets invaluable career advice from industry influencers.

"While safely ensconced in the campus bubble, students are making significant decisions (choosing classes, developing career interests, finding internships) with little 'real' information to go on, save for brightly colored pamphlets from the college career center, tidbits courtesy of the internet, or tips delivered by mentors who have spent the majority of their time in academia. With LinkedIn, in contrast, students can find plenty of information on an industry they are looking to get into as well as the skills and requirements sought in successful candidates, real examples of peoples' career paths, and, if bold enough to ask, answers directly from mainstream professionals — all in one place. It's just a great resource to supplement your education."

Amber makes a great point here. Although your school may offer great services in career placement and professional development, why not go straight to the professionals who are actually working in your field and ask them how they got to where they are today?

**Build Your Credibility as an Expert: Are You up for the Challenge?**
Now, if you feel comfortable enough, take it to the next level and try answering a question. This is your chance to show the world what you have to offer. And again, if you give the best answer, you could build a reputation as an expert on the topic. Over time, by consistently contributing quality answers, you may attract the attention of industry experts. In other words, the more active you are in **Answers**, the more people will view your profile and want to connect with you.

## The Power of the 2nd Degree: Leverage Your Connections to Meet Influencers

As we mentioned before, everyone has hidden connections. For example, when you meet Jason, you have no idea he knows Jacqueline, whom you've heard about but never met. Everyone has a web of connections that aren't apparent until you do some exploration. We assume the people we know have relationships with only a very small segment of the group they actually do know. That's why we rarely think to ask Jason for an introduction to Jacqueline.

There's a psychological principle at work that also prevents us from tapping into these hidden connections. What we call the *horizon of observability* refers to our difficulty in seeing beyond our current connections. If you think of relationships as links on a chain, then we only see the link with whom we're directly connected. In reality, we're connected to many other links, but we don't see them because there's no direct connection. This is where LinkedIn comes in. It allows us to see how we're indirectly connected to others, and gives us the information necessary for discerning whether people are potential connections.

Although LinkedIn makes it easier to see these connections, it's unlikely that you're going to develop *meaningful* relationships with these people inadvertently. You need to take action if you want to explore these relationships. Taking action means establishing deeper relationships with people you do know.

Take the following story for example. When Sonya was completing her master's thesis in psychology she held regular conversations with Tamara, the head of career advising at her graduate school. During one of their long discussions, Tamara explained that she still wanted to get her doctorate, but was waiting until her seven-month-old son was older. This was something Tamara didn't reveal to many people, but she sensed that Sonya would understand. When Sonya was empathetic — her brother's wife had made a similar decision — Tamara opened up more, sharing with Sonya her deep interest in and experience with art. Sonya responded that her sister, Erin, owned an art gallery and would probably be happy to look at Tamara's art.

As they talked, Sonya revealed that although she had considered teaching once she received her master's, what she really wanted to do was open her own private practice. This was a difficult piece of information for Sonya to share, because the dean of the school frowned on graduates starting their own businesses without having worked at a hospital or done some other form of institutional work first. She was worried that Tamara might caution her against this career route, but instead Tamara told her that Carl, who graduated five years earlier, was a good friend of hers and enjoyed a flourishing private practice. In fact, he had called Tamara a few days before and said he was in need of a junior partner. Tamara suggested introducing Sonya to Carl.

From that introduction Sonya established a relationship with Carl that eventually turned into a business alliance. Carl, a brilliant psychologist who had become very influential in the field of child psychology, became Sonya's mentor. It's useful to note that this conversation benefited Tamara as well. Sonya introduced her to Erin, who was impressed by her art and agreed to display her works in the gallery. Figure 5.1 depicts the nature of these existing and newly formed relationships.

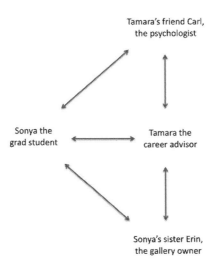

**Figure 5.1 Uncovering Hidden Connections**

Indeed, of all the pathways to influencers, this is the one that is most underutilized. Sometimes all it takes to plug into these hidden connections is an in-depth conversation with someone you know and a willingness to share a significant piece of information about yourself: your career dreams, your values, your fears. In turn, the other person will respond by sharing something that's important to them. In the course of this sharing, you'll not only learn more about that person, but also gain opportunities to access that person's network.

As Tamara and Sonya demonstrated, a significant connection must be established before either person will grant access to their hidden connections. Here you need to earn access, and you can only do that by communicating your values and goals. The benefit is that your current connection will be more interested in giving a thoughtful, compelling introduction and recommendation. Unlike in traditional networking, you actually have a good chance of developing a meaningful relationship with whomever they introduce you to.

This was definitely the case for Joseph O'Brien, who joined LinkedIn about a year before graduating from Williams College in Boston. Joseph was determined to launch his career in the financial services sector by getting a job in private equity. Since he was interested in leaving the Northeast, he realized that it would be difficult to leverage his network – most of his connections were in Boston and New York City and he was targeting firms outside of the United States.

Joseph's close friend Dave worked at a prestigious recruiting firm that specialized in placing pre and post MBAs in private equity positions. One day, Dave informed Joseph about an attractive consulting opportunity in Sydney, Australia. This position was right up his alley so he immediately contacted Dave and submitted his application.

After a few weeks had passed, Joseph had still not heard anything from the firm — he spent countless hours on the web trying to gain all the information he could about the firm. It was not until he decided to go on LinkedIn that he quickly discovered one of the firm's employees was a second-degree connection. LinkedIn revealed that Joseph was connected to this person through three colleagues, all of whom attended his current graduate school. He immediately set up a lunch with Tia (one of the three colleagues) and expressed his passion for private equity and also how he was connected to someone at the Australian firm through her. Since Joseph had a good relationship with Tia, she gladly contacted the inside connection and recommended him for the job. Two months later, he was packing his bags for Syndey and preparing to jump-start his career in private equity in the land down under.

One of the reasons things worked out so well for Joseph was because he was indirectly connected to an influencer. In his case, his colleague Tia was connected to someone who worked at his target company, and this person was able to influence the hiring manager to consider Joseph for the job. There's a good chance that, without LinkedIn, he would not have been able to see this hidden connection. But more importantly, it was Joseph's ability to foster meaningful relaionships and his willingness to explore these relationships further that made the difference.

All the people you know and have formed a bond with have at least one influencer among their hidden connections. In fact, we've found some people who have ten influencers or more. Many times, however, you may be tempted to believe that a current connection begins and ends with that individual. Networlders always take the optimistic, and realistic, point of view that there's an influencer linked to every person.

Because most of us know a lot of people, it's difficult to know whose hidden connections merit seeking out first. To give you a starting point, answer the following questions:

- Who do I know who is most likely to be linked to an influencer?
- Given that person's position, is it reasonable to assume he or she would know influential people?
- Have I heard a friend, family member, colleague, or fellow student talk

about a person in a way that made me think it would be worthwhile to get to know that person, that he or she possesses skills, interests, values, and ideas that overlap with my own?

## Make the Connection: LinkedIn Introductions

LinkedIn offers two great ways to get in touch with new members of your career support network. Whenever you find an influencer with whom you'd like to connect, you should always first try to send them **InMail**. InMail lets you send the person a direct message that appears in their email and LinkedIn inbox. However, there is a catch; to use this feature, you're usually required to upgrade your account.

If LinkedIn does not allow you to send **Inmail**, don't fret. As you continue to build your career support network, you will have more opportunities to make the connection. You can do this by using the **Introductions** feature on LinkedIn.

In the last section, we explained how Sonya, the aspiring psychologist, established a relationship with Carl, the brilliant psychologist who became her mentor. This connection was only made possible by Tamara, the career advisor who introduced Sonya to Carl. In this instance, while Tamara was Sonya's first-degree connection, Carl was her second-degree connection. In the same manner, Joseph's first-degree connection was his colleauge, Tia; his seconed degree connection was the employee at the private equity firm.

How does this relate to LinkedIn? When someone is your first-degree connection, LinkedIn gives you access to *all* of that person's first-degree connections. So in essence, you are only one step away from all of those connections, and that step is made possible by using LinkedIn Introductions. Let's see how Adam leverages this feature.

Adam Carson, a current MBA student at the Tuck School of Business at Dartmouth, uses a connecting style that increases his chances of getting introduced to key influencers. With over 1,200 connections, he's comfortable connecting with anyone he's communicated with in some meaningful way, shape, or form. Also, if he knows the person through someone else, but has not met or spoken with them, he still considers them a connection. Not only does he realize that more connections mean more access to receiving opportunities, but he also likes having more people in his network whom he can provide support:

"I already know who I know; the entire value [of LinkedIn] is derived from the second degree. My network connects me to over 247,000 people through people I know well. These people are otherwise hidden away from my contact lists, rolodex, and even my mind. But regardless of how many connections I have, I still need that trusted connection, the warm introduction that will help me determine if, when, and how I can help or be helped by fostering a deeper relationship."

In Adam's case, he is more open to connecting with someone he doesn't know, but he has to know them through someone he *does* know well before he requests an introduction. Let's see how this actually works on LinkedIn.

### Getting Introduced on LinkedIn

When you locate someone who is a second-degree connection on LinkedIn, all you need to do is view their profile and click the link **Get introduced through a connection**. Next you may see a screen that lists all of your connections who can provide the introduction for you. If you are given this option, choose a person you know well and with whom you have the strongest relationship — this way they will be more likely to provide you with a warmer, more effective introduction.

Once you've chosen your "introducer", you will be prompted to request the introduction by sending messages to both your connection and the person to whom you'd like to meet. Refer to the following screen shot as you read on.

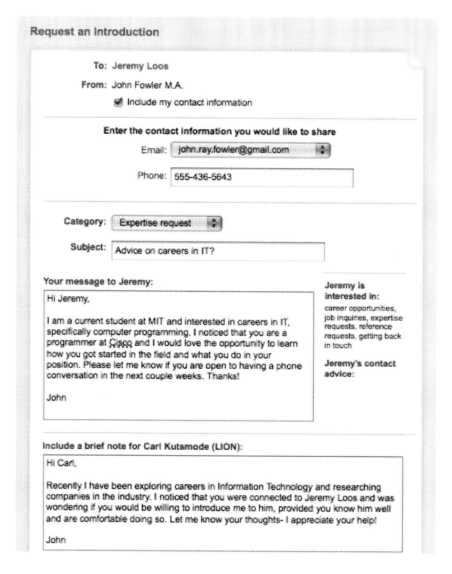

Once you've submitted your request, the message will first reach your connection. Then if they are willing to help, LinkedIn asks them to approve the message before it reaches the other person.

If you don't hear back right away or never at all, it's OK. Some people are very busy, and others don't spend a lot of time on LinkedIn. With that said, sometimes it's best to take the conversation off LinkedIn. It may be more appropriate to ask your connection for the person's contact information so that you can email them directly or call them on the phone.

**Homepage Tip:** Find People You May Know

One of the best places to find second-degree connetions is the People You May Know section on your home page. LinkedIn is pretty smart. You may notice that you recognize some of these names, and better yet, they might be ideal connections because they share the same industry and other points of commonality. Take a look at who you know them through, request a recommendation and make the connection!

During Courtney Dean's job search, she paid special attention to this feature so that she could seek out additional people to connect with. Notice that most, if not all, of these suggestions are second-degree connections. As we've learned, second-degree connections are only an introduction away. By paying attention to these people and where they work, you might just find someone who can help you land your next job.

---

**People You May Know**

**nate jones,** Interactive Marketing Manager at TCS Education System ✕
⊕ Connect

**Lena Parrilli,** M.A. I/O Psychology ✕
⊕ Connect

**Roberto Lopez Tamayo,** Latino Mental Health Providers Network Coordinator at The Chicago School ✕
⊕ Connect

See more »

## Establish Connections with Bridgers

Noted scholars have studied the "people puzzle," or the connections between individuals, since the 1930s. Studies by Yale sociologist Stanley Milgram and mathematicians Steven Strogatz and Duncan Watts concluded that people could connect with any individual in only a few steps using well-placed intermediaries. We call these intermediaries bridgers. They are individuals who bring together people from different groups to develop new opportunities. Just about anyone can be a bridger — a senior executive or your next-door neighbor.

Because of the relationships bridgers cultivate in different areas of their lives, they are invaluable resources in helping you connect with others to achieve your career goals. Bridgers may not provide you directly with opportunities, or even offer you support, but what they will do is link you to others who will become your Networlding partners. They serve an important "middleman" function because both you and the person they help you link up with trust the bridger. This trust makes it easier to explore and establish a relationship with a stranger.

If you can find bridgers in your personal and professional life, they can quickly eliminate whatever degrees of separation exist between you and your desired networking partners. Bridgers are easily identifiable; they're the ones who seem to know everyone, have a knack for anticipating who will work well together, and relish the chance to make introductions. LinkedIn can play an integral role in your ability to find and connect with bridgers, who can then connect you with people who will become part of your career support network.

# Target Industry–Specific Influencers: LinkedIn Advanced People Search

Earlier we touched on how to use LinkedIn's **People Search** to find and connect with your existing contacts. What we didn't show you was how you could use this feature to target specific types of professionals within your field of interest. Katie Andrien, recent graduate of The Chicago School of Professional Psychology, was able to leverage this feature to great success.

After relocating to Halifax, Nova Scotia, Katie launched a new career in health and fitness coaching. Eager to learn more and slightly bewildered by her new environment, Katie knew it would be best to meet another coach in the area. The first thing she did was use the LinkedIn **Advanced People Search** feature to discover relevant individuals. So she searched according to: geographic location, job title, skills, and certifications. (Refer to the following visual to see how she performed this search)

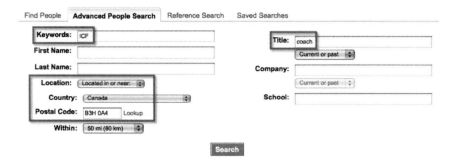

As a result, she was able to find a local coach who not only practiced around the corner, but also shared a similar background. This woman had extensive experience coaching at a variety of levels, performing workshops and speaking at seminars. But most important was her eagerness to meet with Katie, share stories, and build a friendship. Several months later, they continued to work together trading services and ideas. Without LinkedIn, Katie would never have met this mentor who helped her grow as a coach and uncover business opportunities.

Potential connection or mentor?

# Networlding Tip:
## Approach and Interact with Influencers on LinkedIn

Simply entering keywords using Google or another search engine can lead you to experts in any industry you choose. Once you've identified an influencer online, research his or her profile and look for something that this individual has done that touches you emotionally as well as intellectually. Email or message the person to support those ideas. If you present yourself genuinely and specifically point out things you appreciate about him or her, this influencer may respond in a positive manner, or at least be more receptive to your message.

LinkedIn is a great place to reach influencers because they will treat you as an equal, and you are less likely to be intimidated by their reputation (as you might be if you met in person). Additionally, the Internet can help you cross geographical boundaries to meet influencers. You may live in a small town, but suddenly you have access to an influencer in a big city. The internet provides you with unprecedented access to all types of influencers.

**Homepage Tip:** Monitor Network Updates for New Connections

Sorted in chronological order, your **Network Updates** feed displays the latest activity of your connections. You'll find things such as their current status, groups recently joined, questions asked and answered, and who they've recently connected to.

If you have connections who share lots of content (too much) in your **Network Updates** stream, you can hide those connections from view in order to keep your stream relevant to your interests. Just roll over an update and click Hide. If you change your mind, you can always restore those updates with just a click. This function provides a great way to filter and curate your news feed for information that is truly useful to you.

Here are some additional facets to keep in mind:
- Clicking on a group name in your updates will bring you to the page to join that group.
- Hovering over a person's name will bring up a summary of their profile; clicking on it will take you to their profile.
- You can control the type and number of notifications that appear in your **Network Updates** feed in your settings.

# Initiating Exchanging Relationships: Paying it Forward

# CHAPTER 6

# Initiating Exchanging Relationships: Paying it Forward

Whether you're attempting to establish Networlding relationships with people you know or with people you want to know, you need to take the initiative. Even basic networking isn't effective if you sit around hoping someone else will make contact. However, initiating Networlding relationships requires more than exchanging business cards or making phone calls. As we've already seen, the prerequisite for Networlding is a relationship exchange. Your objective is to establish relationships with mutual exchange as the foundation.

Perhaps the most challenging part of the exchange process is the fear that you have little if anything to give, especially as a college student or young professional. It's important to overcome this fear, and one way of doing so is to think about all the exchanges you've made throughout your life. As a high school student, you repeatedly exchanged your homework for a grade. In any work setting, you exchanged your work for income. Every day you exchange information, ideas, and feelings with others. Consciously or not, you have a long and continuous history of making exchanges. In this section, we're simply going to show you how to become more conscious of this exchange process.

The most important skill to learn in Networlding is the skill of exchanging. You give something of value in anticipation of something of equal or greater value. You continuously work to educate members of your career support network so that they are thoroughly aware of your interests and needs. It is in these ongoing exchanges that we realize the potential of

Networlding. When we exchange in an environment of trust and interest, we are free to create connections that have maximum benefit for both parties.

## Discover What you Have to Offer: The Networlding Support Exchange Model Revisited

Initiating relationships becomes easier when you realize that you're not coming into it empty-handed. The Networlding support exchange model was introduced in Chapter 1 where we briefly mentioned the types of support people exchange with each other. Here, we'd like to go into more depth about this so that you'll be in a better position to make these exchanges when you begin to make a connection. Although exchanges can be formalized — they can involve a significant amount of time, thought, and discussion — the ones that you'll use initially are more informal. You and another person will not meet for the first time and immediately begin providing each other with every possible form of support in order to pursue major opportunities. Nevertheless, unlike an initial networking contact, you should try to give something in exchange right from the start.

The support exchange model mirrors the hierarchical process involved in building any meaningful relationship. We've simply translated it into a tool that you can refer to in building successful exchanges. Let's look at the types of support used to initiate effective relationships so you have a better idea on what you have to contribute.

### Emotional Support

Just because you don't know someone well or are interacting with that person in an academic or business environment doesn't mean you should do so without any significant emotional giving. Some people feel it's "unprofessional" to reveal feelings within the work context or to allow a conversation to "descend" to that level, but it's actually the best way to push the relationship beyond a superficial state, even if it's with professors or experienced professionals.

Best-selling author Daniel Goleman's book *Working with Emotional Intelligence* refers to almost five hundred independent studies that support the importance of emotional intelligence (the ability to understand emotions and use them to promote emotional and intellectual growth in oneself and others). It's this same intelligence that exists at the foundation of all the relationships we build. It's this chemistry, or lack of it, that starts or stops a relationship between two people. Possessing soft skills, such as empathy, is just as important as possessing purely technical skills.

Increasingly, people are receptive to emotional honesty and are looking for someone who not only says what he or she really feels, but is also an empathic listener. An exchange of emotional support is a signal that you care about another person (and not just the work). It's very common for students and young professionals like you to initiate relationships with older influencers simply by being attentive, responsive listeners. That doesn't mean that you can build a relationship by pretending to listen, but if you express honest interest and concern, verbally or through body language, people will react positively.

Giving praise unexpectedly is also a good initiating technique. Telling people how much you appreciate what they've done when they don't expect can build powerful bonds. This can't be routine however; the surprise makes the other person think: "I didn't realize that Mary understood how hard I fought for her transfer," or "Gilbert really gets that it was my persistence and ideas that helped the team achieve its goal." When the praise is routine — a thank you for a raise, or a show of appreciation at the successful conclusion of a project — the impact isn't as great.

## Homepage Tip:
### Building Your Professional Brand by Sharing

As a professional or student, you commonly share news articles, events, and business intelligence with your colleagues or classmates. LinkedIn's sharing feature is an easy way for you to take this routine action to your connections online. You can quickly and easily share links, articles, and more with your connections and fellow group members. Use sharing to:

- Update your professional network about new developments in your career.
- Share links to news articles, events, ideas, or job openings.
- Click the **Twitter** box to share your updates with your followers on Twitter.

Of course, we're not suggesting that you become sloppily sentimental, but when you encounter someone who seems to share your values, who is an influencer, and who has goals that overlap with your own, then doing this may be a good way to initiate a relationship. Don't hesitate to provide emotional support to your connections by sending them messages of encouragement or appreciation on LinkedIn.

### Informational Support

We live in the information age, and it's not uncommon to become overwhelmed by all the data out there. So the key here isn't simply to offer easily accessible or obvious information. A relationship should be initiated with valuable information. If you provide someone with eye-opening facts and useful statistics that are normally difficult to find, their perception of you will change. It's as if you've become that person's private, highly effective market research firm.

Exchanging informational support does require some time and preparation. You may have the world at your fingertips if you're good at pulling information from the internet, but you need to exercise your analytical skills to glean additional value from the facts, as well as determine what's important to each particular individual. For example, if you know that one of your classmates is doing a presentation on social media marketing, an ideal source of information for you to share could be a business article, white paper, or industry report — something you might have found on LinkedIn from one of your connections. Once you get more comfortable with LinkedIn's sharing capabilities, the easier it will be to provide informational support.

## Knowledge Support

There's a subtle but important difference between informational support and knowledge support. Informational support involves sharing pure data; knowledge support involves sharing one's conclusions, hypotheses, and the like. The knowledge shared is based upon experience, not just visible information. Those who receive it are impressed by someone's willingness to part with such hard-won knowledge, and it provides the leverage to move a new relationship to a higher level. A prime example would be a college senior sharing knowledge regarding classes and internships with a college junior. The key is, you've been through the process before and have an educated perspective on how to approach the situation because of your experience.

## Promotional Support

Perhaps the best way to get a Networlding relationship off on the right foot is to hot-link one person to another. Hot linking involves consciously seeking opportunities to promote the strengths of people in your primary circle — the ones whom you know best and with whom you have the strongest relationships. By consciously keeping an eye out for connections between people, you put yourself in a position to bridge your connections to new opportunities, thereby providing invaluable promotional support. You don't have to be an influencer to provide this type of support. All it takes is a high level of awareness and the initiative to refer or introduce your connections to one another.

Promotional support spreads quickly from one person to the next. When you inform Jake that Heather is absolutely terrific at particular skills that he's been looking for, Jake is likely not only to call Heather but also to mention her to someone else who needs her skills. This form of support is called "word-of-mouth marketing" and, as you probably know, it's the most effective form of marketing. Networlders recognize its power and use it to create opportunities for themselves and for the people whom they promote.

Promotional support is practically an automatic reaction among Networlders. They are always saying things like this to people in their various circles: "You should meet Pam. She's the most gifted graphic designer I've ever seen. You might consider using her on your next project." Or, "You have to take Dr. Ackly for Organizational Consulting next semester. He not only has an engaging teaching style, but he is also highly experienced in the field and has helped many students find jobs after they graduate."

As you promote, so too are you promoted. This crucial exchange is one you want to establish from the very beginning of a relationship. In many ways, it's a good test of the relationship's quality. If you promote someone to others, will he or she promote you back? Promotional support works in all sorts of ways. It not only helps you establish a relationship with the individual you're supporting, but also gets your name out there. Once you build a reputation as someone who promotes others, you'll be amazed at the opportunities that result.

A great example of a support exchange is the way Ty Bennett runs his business. Ty Bennett is the founder of Leadership Inc., a speaking and training company dedicated to empowering individuals and organizations. As a speaker, author, and entrepreneur Ty has acheived success at a very young age — 21. He accomplished this by actively engaging in multiple types of exchanges and as a result, these efforts have been re-ciprocated continuously. Because Ty provided the emotional and knowl-edge support his audience needed to be successful, his clients rewarded him with promotional support, leads, and referrals that resulted in an increase in speaking engagements and training sessions. Some of Ty's most loyal fans created awareness of his programs on Twitter, LinkedIn, and other social networking sites, leading to even more exposure.

These types of support exchanges make it infinitely easier to develop opportunities with others. In networking, one or both networkers often shy away from opportunities because they feel that they're imposing or being imposed upon. People know when they're using others or being used. Networlding, however, involves a concious effort on both sides to look for opportunities to provide support.

## Provide Support for Your Connections on LinkedIn: Write Recommendations

One of the best ways you can provide promotional support for members of your network is to write recommendations for them on LinkedIn. If you recall the guidelines we provided for requesting recommendations, the same should apply when you decide to endorse one of your connections.

There are two ways upon which you can write a recommendation: 1) you receive a message in your **Inbox** from a connection asking you to en-dorse them or 2) you take the time to write a recommendation for some-one who has not asked to be endorsed.

In the first scenario, you have to make a decision whether you feel comfortable recommending that person (remember discernment?) This is where you ask yourself, "How well do I know this person? Have I worked with them in some professional capacity? Am I able to speak to the quality and nature of their work? Do I have good things to say about them?" If you're not sure you can answer these questions, then perhaps you should not write this person a recommendation.

The second scenario has the potential to be more rewarding. In other words, you actually take the time to think about those in your network whom you value and respect; you then take the time to compose a thought-out, well-written statement about them and their work. You highlight their key strengths, strongest qualities, and unique characteristics. As a result, you provide for them a public endorsement that not only speaks highly of and promotes your connection, but also showcases your respect and appreciation for members of your network.

Once you have crafted a high quality recommendation, you can then visit their profile and click **Recommend this person**. Next, LinkedIn prompts you to recommend the person as a Colleague, Service Provider, Business Partner, or Student. Now you're ready to create your endorsement by choosing the basis of the relationship and pasting your pre-written recommendation into the provided space. The following screen shot is a prime example of a well-written recommendation.

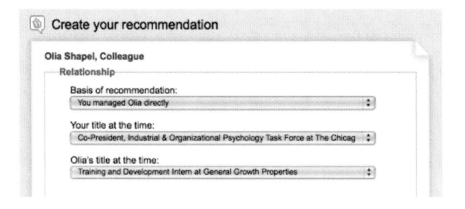

Written Recommendation

Write a brief recommendation for Olia. Recommendations you write will appear on your profile.

I worked with Olia in our graduate school's student organization. She not only took her role as Alumni Relations Coordinator seriously, but she also looked for alternate ways to lead and contribute to the team. Olia teamed up with me to develop a Peer Mentoring Program that connected over 100 graduate students. She played an integral role in the project because of her strategic planning, project management, and outstanding communication skills.

Whether she's tackling volunteer work or spear-heading a consulting project, Olia has the innate ability to recognize when to lead and when to collaborate in order to accomplish a common goal. In addition, she consistently delivers a quality product, always going above and beyond the expectations of her colleagues and supervisors. There is no doubt in my mind that Olia will be successful wherever her career takes her.

As we conclude this chapter, we hope to leave you with the understanding that initiating a relationship can quickly lead to an exchange that goes beyond ideas, facts, and emotional support. It can also lead to long-term relationships and transformational opportunities. As you work on forming your primary circle and then expanding your circles over time, it's important to realize that although you may still be in college or in the early stages of your career, you have much to offer your network. The more conscious you are about seeking out mutual exchanges, the more meaningful and fruitful your career support network will be.

# Jump–starting Your Job Search with LinkedIn

# Jump-starting Your Job Search with LinkedIn

In the "Foreward", we shared with you how this book started as a partnership between John and Melissa, two professionals who quickly formed a bond by discovering that they shared the same values and passions. Indeed, these interactions were made possible by the power and accessibility that social media provides. By looking at John's LinkedIn profile, Melissa was able to discern John's potential as a Networlding partner and co-author; she noticed that he had previous experience creating and delivering LinkedIn workshops. What she didn't know, however, was how John started doing LinkedIn workshops in the first place. Amazingly enough, the answer to this question is, again, LinkedIn.

During John's last semester of graduate school, he jump-started his job search by choosing a few industries and compiling a list of target companies within each of those industries. Since he had a passion for career development, mentoring and coaching, this list included a number of talent management and human captital consulting firms. So what did he do next? He went to LinkedIn and researched these companies to learn more about their offerings and also to see if he knew any existing employees. After conducting a **Companies** search for Lee Hecht Harrison, he quickly saw that he was not connected directly to any current employees, but he was connected to a former one. John couldn't believe his eyes. The person he was connected to was Julie, the Career Services Director of his own graduate school!

Right away, John sent her an email requesting to meet and discuss her career at Lee Hecht Harrison, as well any other advice she might have about the field. Julie happily agreed and, before he knew it, John was in her office talking about his interest in career coaching as well as his appreciation for how integral LinkedIn had been during his job search. Once Julie saw John's passion for LinkedIn and for showing others how to use it strategically, she asked him if he would be interested in creating a workshop for the students. Not only was this a great opportunity for John, but this was the beginning of a long-term relationship full of mutual exchanges. It wasn't too long before he started delivering these workshops at other schools, building experience as a speaker and gaining additional expertise in LinkedIn.

If it wasn't for Julie's offer, John might never have explored the potential of specializing in LinkedIn training, much less acquired the knowledge, skills, and experience Melissa was looking for in a co-author. The point of this story is simple: if you learn to use the Networlding approach to LinkedIn, you will increase your chances of finding jobs and opportunities for career development. In John's case, his opportunity was sparked by a simple search using the **Companies** feature on LinkedIn and completed by a meaningful, exchange-filled relationship.

## Homepage Tip:
### Set Your LinkedIn Home Page as Your Browser Home Page

Many of you have probably heard the old adage "Treat your job search like a full-time job." Finding the job you really want takes time and effort. As you will discover, however, LinkedIn can save you so much time finding and connecting with the right people who can help you get that job. One thing you can do to get off on the right foot is to set LinkedIn as the home page on your internet browser so it's the first thing you see each day during your job search. Doing so will make you more aware of potential opportunities in your career support network.

As you can probably tell by John's story, opportunities present themselves in unique ways. There is no single approach that guarantees you will find that next project, internship, or career opportunity. Success will only come when you make a consious effort to build meaningful connections with the right people.

## Focus on Companies and People, and the Jobs Will Follow

There are only two ways to get a job — you look for the employer yourself or the employer looks for you. The latter occurs when companies post job advertisements, job postings on careerbuilder.com (or other sites) and job postings on company websites. This is called the advertised job market, a world where most of us are comfortable; it simply makes sense to look in places where you know jobs already exist. But the advertised job market is frustrating and slow for both the employer and the applicant. For the applicant, it means lots of competition — particularly for entry-level positions (those of which most of you will be targeting upon graduation). You know the drill. You find a job posting online and submit a resume and cover letter, hoping you match the employer's requirements. The fact of the matter is, the advertised job market is only a tiny fraction of available jobs. More often than not, the best career opportunities are never advertised to the public.

The other type of job market is commonly referred to as the "hidden" job market, a world where positions are filled by or created for candidates who come to an employer's attention through employee recommendations, referrals from trusted associates, recruiters, or direct contact with the candidate. Believe it or not, 80 percent of all positions are in the hidden job market. These jobs are filled *without* employer advertising. Successful hidden job market candidates are able to connect with the employer's network. For example, the candidate comes "pre-recommended" by someone the employer trusts (remember Joseph O'Brien's story?). The key to the hidden job market is your career support network, and, as we've mentioned repeatedly, LinkedIn is best tool you can use to tap into your network and discover these hidden opportunities.

If most jobs are not advertised, then how are employers finding and attracting candidates? As of August 2009, 40 percent of Fortune 100 companies were using LinkedIn to source and hire candidates. The number of companies using LinkedIn and other forms of social media to recruit talent is on the rise. Companies are learning that LinkedIn's ability to help them find and hire top passive candidates saves them significant amounts of money traditionally spent on third party (staffing) agencies and job boards. LinkedIn members come from 130 different industries, and include 130,000 recruiters. Some companies, believe it or not, will only consider those candidates who have managed to tap into their network to learn about job openings. It's gotten to the point where it's practically considered unprofessional to not be on LinkedIn!

Take Lyndi Horn's story for example. After Lyndi graduated with her master's degree from The Chicago School of Professional Psychology, her primary goal was to find a recruiting position and relocate to Austin, Texas. Lyndi's friend and former classmate Jamie had already moved to Austin and secured a job. One day a recruiter reached out to Jamie via LinkedIn to see if she'd be interested in a recruiting opporuntity; keeping in mind that Lyndi was interested in recruiting, Jamie used LinkedIn to introduce the recruiter to Lyndi. After several online interactions, Lyndi was asked to come in for an interview and, next thing she knew, she landed the job and was making arrangements to relocate to Austin!

"It actually kind of fell into my lap, however, without LinkedIn I wouldn't have gotten the chance to interview since my new company doesn't post recruiting jobs on their website. Instead, they recruit people through social media and professional networks."

Hopefully it's now clear to you that most jobs are not within reach in the traditional sense. The best jobs and opportunities are seemingly invisible and the only way to find them is connecting to the people within the companies you're targeting. Does this mean that we discourage you from looking for jobs on Monster.com, Indeed.com and other online job boards? No, but we are suggesting that you focus your job search more on people and companies, not just job postings. Next we will cover four ways you can use LinkedIn to conduct your job search. Just keep in mind that success does not depend on one particular approach, it depends on the size of your career support network and the quality of your relationships.

## Four Ways to Use LinkedIn to Find Career Opportunities

1. **Get Jobs and Opportunities to Find You**
2. **Research Companies**
3. **Research People**
4. **Find Jobs (with LinkedIn)**

### 1. Get Jobs and Opportunities to Find You

Wouldn't it be great if you could just sit back and let the jobs come to you? If you think this idea sounds too good to be true, you're right. You can, however, increase the chances that an opportunity will find you. The good news is, if you've followed each step of the Networlding approach to LinkedIn, then you've already set yourself up to receive opportunities. The following section presents more nuanced detail for getting noticed on LinkedIn.

IS YOUR PROFILE COMPLETE?

In *Crafting Your Profile on LinkedIn*, we emphasized that having a 100 percent complete profile increases your chances to receive opportunities on LinkedIn. Take this moment to revisit your profile and make sure you've included the following components:

- At least one current position
- At least two past positions
- Your college (education)
- A profile summary
- A profile photo
- Your specialties
- At least three recommendations

Again, if you find yourself at 85 percent completeness, it's probably because you haven't received any recommendations from members of your career support network. This is when you should think about the people who know you well and have worked with you, in any context. Getting endorsed by three people will get you to 100 percent profile completeness.

### ARE YOU COMMUNICATING YOUR PROFESSIONAL BRAND?

Next, revisit your profile to see if you are clearly communicating your professional brand. Make sure you:

- Speak to what you've done, what you currently do, and who you aspire to be.
- Create a headline that defines you as a professional, not just your title or the organization you work for.
- Communicate in your summary and specialties how you can add value to a project, organization, or profession. Why would a potential employer or business partner choose you?
- Use keywords in your summary and specialties relevant to your industry or occupation so that people can find you on the web.
- Convey to your audience who you are as a person. What are your values and passions? What drives you to succeed?

SHOW OFF YOUR WORK WITH LINKEDIN APPLICATIONS

Another way to enhance your profile and attract the attention of prospective employers is to showcase your work. Using LinkedIn applications, you can add examples of your writing, design work, or any other document that conveys your accomplishments. You can access applications by hovering your mouse over **More...** on the toolbar at the top of the page; then click **Application Directory**. We recommend Box.net Files, SlideShare Presentations, and Google Presentations. All of these applications allow you to upload and share content with your network. For example, you may have an excellent PowerPoint presentation you created for a class or a research paper you wrote in graduate school; including your best work within your profile is the equivalent of bringing your professional portfolio to a job interview. Impress recruiters before they even get a chance to call you in.

Have a website or a blog that showcases your work? Make this information viewable on your profile by adding WordPress or BlogLink. These applications allow you to sync your blogs so that when you add new content to your blog, your LinkedIn profile is also updated.

MAKE THE MOST OF YOUR VANITY URL

Courtney Dean, recent graduate of the University of North Carolina, attributes much of her success in getting potential employers' attention (and job interviews) to her solid LinkedIn profile. She gets their attention by leveraging her vanity URL. In *Crafting Your Profile on LinkedIn*, we explained how LinkedIn assigns you a customizable URL; what we did not discuss was how this URL could be used to drive people to your profile. There are a few ways we recommend you leverage your URL. The first strategy is to include it on your resume like Courtney does:

"I cannot pinpoint exactly what landed me my current job or past internships, but my current employer's HR representative did point out to me during my interviews that they had viewed my LinkedIn profile. I'm also now connected with this representative on LinkedIn. I'd always included my LinkedIn profile URL on my resume for every job and internship that I applied for. My view is that employers have come to expect to be able to find perspective employees on LinkedIn."

Courtney also includes her URL on other online professional profiles, such as her Visual CV (a great website devoted to online resumes). Another helpful site is KODA, a social recruiting platform designed for more personal interaction between candidates and employers. When you create a profile on KODA, you can use your URL to attract others. We also recommend including your URLs as links on your Twitter and Facebook profiles.

Finally, you may also consider listing your vanity URL along with the other contact information included in your email signature or business card.

Presenting your URL in these ways not only encourages others to visit your profile, but sometimes is actually enough to get them to connect — yet another way to add connections to your career support network.

**GET THE WORD OUT WITH STATUS UPDATES**

If you're on Facebook or Twitter, then you're already familiar with status updates. Status updates are a perfect way to get the word out about your job search to everyone in your career support network. Each time you update your status, you're literally broadcasting a message to your connections. If you thought no one was listening, you'd be surprised.

While Chris Stewart was wrapping up his MBA at the University of Denver, his goal was to target the renewable energies industry and look for "green" jobs. With the help of a friend, Chris discovered a job opportunity online that seemed right up his alley. However, he still wanted to get the inside scoop about the position, the corporate culture, and the key decision makers. The first thing he did was update his LinkedIn status to "Chris is looking to connect with employees working at..."

Within days, he received two responses to his status update. One response was from a former co-worker and the other from a former classmate. His former co-worker was able to put him in touch with the Director of Human Resources, a key decision maker for the job in question. What's more amazing though is that his former classmate actually knew the person who used to have the job! After a proper introduction, Chris had the opportunity to speak with the former employee and learn specific details about the company and the position he was applying for.

Needless to say, Chris easily got the chance to interview for the position. He became a top-three finalist and, although he never completed the interview process (he ended up taking another job), he was quite grateful to have such a supportive network of people who were willing to help. He realized that he probably wouldn't have gotten the chance to interview if it wasn't for LinkedIn, and it all started with a status update.

Status updates are more than just telling people what you're doing, they're an opportunity for you to let people know what you're working on and to share professional information with your career support network. What project are you working on in school or at work? What are you reading or studying? Where are you traveling to for work? What conferences are you attending?

When it comes to the job search, don't be afraid to announce to your network that you're seeking jobs or career opportunities. If you choose to go this route, just make sure you're as specific as possible. There's a huge difference between "Jacqueline is looking for a job" and "Jacqueline is seeking career opportunities with management consulting firms in New York." Being clear about what you're looking for encourages people with the perfect match to help you out. Here are some more tips for getting the word out with status updates:

DO:

- Keep it professional and relevant to your work, your job, and your career.
- Let your network know that you're seeking career opportunities
- Share links to blogs, articles, news, and events that are professional, interesting, and informative.
- Ask questions and make comments that are engaging and invite conversation.

DON'T:

- Share personal or intimate details about yourself or others.
- Beg your network for job leads or come across as desperate in your job search.
- Share links to inappropriate or offensive websites, blogs, or articles.
- Ask questions and make comments that invite negative or defensive responses.

---

### Homepage Tip: Check Your Updates

When Maria Bakardjieva (recent MBA graduate of European University) went to study abroad in Spain, she interviewed with several companies only to fall short of getting a job. She did, however, feel confident enough about the connection she had with one of her interviewers to connect with him on LinkedIn and make an effort to stay in touch. Months later, Maria noticed on her LinkedIn home page that the interviewer updated his status to "So much work and so little time." Still unemployed, Maria capitalized on this opportunity by posting a comment asking him if there was anything she could do to help. Next thing she knew, he had asked her to come in to discuss whether she could be a good fit for a fresh, new project. Three interviews later, she got the job. How's that for a Networlder!

HOW DO YOU FEEL ABOUT YOUR NETWORK?

One of the coolest things about LinkedIn is that it enables you to view valu-able information about your career support network. You can access this information by hovering over **Contacts** and selecting **Network Statistics** (Your page should look like the next two screen shots). Now you have a snapshot of your network highlighting key statistics such as:

• The total number of 1st, 2nd, and 3rd degree connections

• The top cities and regions of which your network gives you access

• The top industries of which your network gives you access

This information will become especially important as you start making decisions about your target jobs, companies, and industries (which we will discuss later in this section). Keep tabs on what kind of representa-tion your network gives you. Every six months or so go back to your network and survey it. Where are the gaps? Look for diverse networks. Go out of your usual set of networking connections. For example, if you enjoy running marathons, join a runner's network. Why? You will meet a lot of great influencers who are not in your industry but because of that provide a rare opportunity to get connections that many other in your industry would never think of getting.

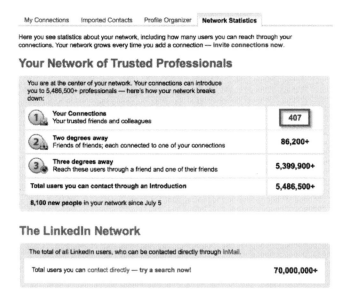

Keeping track of your network is important because you never know when you might lose your job or decide to move into another industry. Finding more general networks where influencers participate will help you. You will have built a group of trusted professional friends who will be right at your fingertips.

Melissa has learned the value of tracking her network and making sure she targeted, yet diverse representation. She has been working with 6 Figure Jobs as their networking coach for more than seven years and continued to talk with top executives who share the same story. "I can't believe this happened to me," they say, "I never thought I would be out of a job. My field is not the place to be right now. How can I make a transition into another field?"

Building your career support network early and monitoring its status on a regular basis will give you a sense of security and stability in your career and in your life.

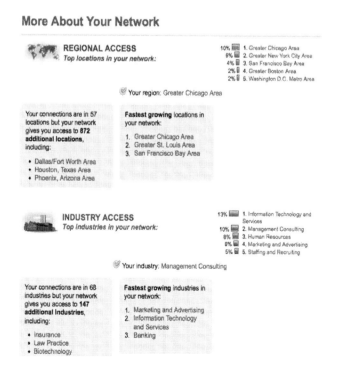

### More About Your Network

**REGIONAL ACCESS**
*Top locations in your network:*

10% 1. Greater Chicago Area
8% 2. Greater New York City Area
4% 3. San Francisco Bay Area
2% 4. Greater Boston Area
2% 5. Washington D.C. Metro Area

Your region: Greater Chicago Area

Your connections are in 57 locations but your network gives you access to **872 additional locations,** including:

- Dallas/Fort Worth Area
- Houston, Texas Area
- Phoenix, Arizona Area

**Fastest growing** locations in your network:

1. Greater Chicago Area
2. Greater St. Louis Area
3. San Francisco Bay Area

**INDUSTRY ACCESS**
*Top industries in your network:*

13% 1. Information Technology and Services
10% 2. Management Consulting
8% 3. Human Resources
8% 4. Marketing and Advertising
5% 5. Staffing and Recruiting

Your industry: Management Consulting

Your connections are in 68 industries but your network gives you access to **147 additional industries,** including:

- Insurance
- Law Practice
- Biotechnology

**Fastest growing** industries in your network:

1. Marketing and Advertising
2. Information Technology and Services
3. Banking

**Homepage Tip:** Who's Viewed My Profile?

This feature can be quite interesting, especially if you've got a killer profile that has the potential to attract recruiters and hiring managers. Not only does it tell you how many times you've recently appeared in search results, but it also gives you a way to benchmark the attention you're generating within your network. Pay attention to the specific individuals who have viewed your profile. You just might find that you're being sized up for a career opportunity.

Who's Viewed My Profile

What is this?  Edit Visibility Settings

Your profile has been viewed by **5 people** in the last day, including:

Jeff Bailey, PhD, Someone from CherryRoad Technologies

Someone in the Leadership function in the Internet industry from San Francisco Bay Area

Analyst at Accenture

Someone at Fundata Canada Inc.

Someone at Accenture

Linked**in**.

To see the full list of **who viewed your profile** and more...

Upgrade Now!

WHAT IF JOBS AND OPPORTUNITIES DON'T FIND ME?

We just uncovered some great ways you can use LinkedIn to attract potential employers and business partners. By building a 100 percent complete profile, communicating your brand effectively, and leveraging various applications and features, you are able to increase the chances that jobs and opportunities will find you. Although setting yourself up for success in this manner could help you land a job, please realize we are not suggesting you sit around and wait for something to fall into your lap. Most likely, you will not be able to find a job using this approach alone, especially in a highly competitive job market. In the next section, we will explain how you can be proactive in your job search by using LinkedIn to research companies.

## 2. Research Companies

One of the best ways to conduct a successful job search is to target specific organizations. As we learned earlier, John might not have found his Career Services Director, Julie, if he didn't use LinkedIn to research her former company — one that was on his list of targeted organizations. In *Crafting Your Profile on LinkedIn* we mentioned that Eric Kuhn started building his profile during his junior year and built connections that led to an internship. What we didn't mention is how he used LinkedIn **Companies** to find an inside connection within one of his target companies.

In fact, when Lauren McCabe (recent graduate of Northwestern University) sees a job posting online, the first place she goes is LinkedIn to find and research the company to see if she knows anyone inside. She feels that in this economy, it's easy to get lost in the mix when applying blindly to jobs; she only applies to positions with companies where she has an "in". The best way to find out if she has an "in" is by performing a **Companies** search on LinkedIn..

In this section, we'll give you an overview of the **Companies** feature, followed by an approach we recommend for conducting your job search based on your top-ten list of targeted companies.

### LINKEDIN COMPANIES

LinkedIn **Companies** allows you to find and research the organizations you're interested in working for or doing business with. Think of it as your portal to a virtual Yellow Pages — a company directory giving you powerful information about different companies and, most importantly, the people who work there. Let's take a look.

Clicking on the **Companies** option on your top navigation bar takes you to the **Companies Home page**. LinkedIn gives you three ways to search for companies. First, if you already know the name of the company, you can enter it into the search field and LinkedIn will take you to the company profile page. Second, there's a keyword search option which allows you to search for a company using industry-related keywords. You can also search for companies on a geographic basis, by country, state, or postal code.

Finally, by selecting **More options...** you can search using more advanced criteria such as company size and industry. If you're wondering how LinkedIn categorizes different industries, simply click **Browse Industries**.

(You can also access company profile pages through a person's profile. When viewing a LinkedIn member profile, the ⊡ icon next to a company name indicates that there is data available for that company; clicking on the name will take you to their company profile.)

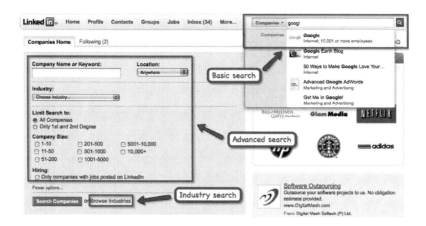

Once you find the company you're looking for, LinkedIn will direct you to the company profile page. Company profiles provide general information about the company and its specialties. In addition, they give you access to employee profiles as well as aggregated statistics about these employees. Here's a brief overview of the key components and things to consider when researching companies during your job search.

OVERVIEW

Why sort through all the clutter of a company website when you have the most important information readily available on LinkedIn? When you arrive at a company's profile page, the first thing you see is a brief overview of the company followed by a list of its specialities. When you scroll down and look to the right, you will then see basic information about the company such as its type, size, website, industry, and headquarters location — all key things to know when researching your target companies.

Finally, keep your eye out for companies with job listings. Next to **Overview**, you will sometimes see a link for a **Careers** tab. You will always want to check this portion of the company profile to see if there are any relevant job postings. You never know when the right job will be waiting for you.

STATISTICS

When it comes to company information, LinkedIn takes it to the next level by providing detailed statistics about a company's growth, job functions, and job titles. Access this data by clicking the link on the top right entitled **Check out insightful statistics about [company name] employees >>**.

Not only can you see how the company has grown on LinkedIn over time, but also you can see the composition of a comany's employee base, including stats about the employees' job functions, educational degree, years of experience, and university attended. This is invaluable information you can use when researching your dream companies. Check out the following graph showing the most common universities attended by Google employees. It helps to know if a significant number of employees working for your target company hired people from your university. In this case, being a student at Stanford might give you the upper hand if you want to work at Google, especially if it means they're active recruiters on your campus; or perhaps you might know a Stanford alum who could help you get your foot in the door.

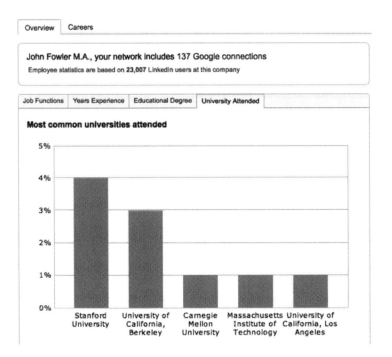

## PEOPLE AND CONNECTIONS

The most powerful information on the company profile, in our opinion, is the list of LinkedIn users in your network who currently work for the company. This list is viewable when you click the **Your Network tab**. People listed first are direct members of your career support network — your first-degree connections. LinkedIn then lists your second-degree, third-degree, and group connections.

When viewing the employees within your targeted company profile, it's important to consider who these people are and how closely you're connected to them. In the next section, "Research People", we will go into detail about targeting potential champions who can help you get the job.

Next to **Your Network** there's a table called **New Hires**. This section can be quite enlightening if you're wondering whether the company is actually hiring. **New Hires** are LinkedIn users who have recently indicated in their profile that they've joined the company. Although people don't always update their profile in real-time as soon as they join a company, you can still get a pretty good idea. For instance, consider this: if some-one told you that Google was on a hiring freeze, we'd be a little skeptical since there appears to be a fair number of recent new hires.

Of course, another way to tell if a company is hiring is to check for job postings on the company profile. Even better, when you conduct your company search by keyword, click on **See more...** and check the box called **Only Companies with Jobs Posted on LinkedIn**.

### SOCIAL MEDIA ACTIVITY

Aside from employee statistics and company information, company profiles on LinkedIn are tightly integrated with the activity that is taking place on Twitter, the company blog, and within the LinkedIn company profile page itself.

For example, on the Google company profile you will see tabs labeled **Recent Tweets** and **Recent Blog Posts**. Periodically monitoring this activity will keep you informed of news, events, or job opportunities for your target companies. You can also scroll below this section to view **[company name] Activity on LinkedIn** to see if what updates have been made to the page, including new job postings.

Now we realize that we've presented you with a lot of information about LinkedIn company profiles. What's most important to remember is: if you focus your job search on a managable list of target companies, it will be easier and less time-consuming to perform your research. In the next section we will cover our approach to keeping your job search focused on the companies that matter most to you — your top-ten list.

## Homepage Tip:
### Follow Companies

Not only can you follow individuals on LinkedIn, there's a feature of LinkedIn that also allows you to follow companies you admire. Once you follow them you will get updates. Like watching stocks on the stock exchange, these will help you find companies that are hiring. Even if you are currently employed somewhere else, this option will provide you with great info on what is going in at other companies where you might someday work. Updates about your companies show up on your home page under **Company Updates.**

CREATE YOUR TOP-TEN LIST OF TARGETED COMPANIES

Before you begin searching for companies on LinkedIn, we recommend taking a focused approach and constructing a top-ten list. This list will help you prioritize your efforts and increase the productivity of your time spent on LinkedIn.

First, think about common job titles or job functions describing the type of role you're interested in. For example, let's say you are a marketing major looking for your first job out of college. Target job titles may include "marketing assistant", "marketing associate", or "marketing coordinator". If you're unsure of example job titles, check out O*NET Online (http://online.onetcenter.org/) and perform an occupation search.

Second, make a list of the top three industries you'd like to work in. Let's say you're most fascinated by the food and beverage industry, specifically soda and beer companies. You're also curious about working in consumer goods. And finally, it makes sense for you to target the marketing and advertising industry. If you have trouble thinking of industries, use LinkedIn **Companies** and the **Browse Industries** option to get ideas.

Lastly, decide where you'd like to live. If you have family in Dallas and have always been interested in living in Austin or San Antonio, you now have your top three geographic preferences.

Once you've completed these three steps (job titles, industries, locations), you now have the criteria for creating your top-ten list of targeted companies. But how do you actually find companies according to this criteria? LinkedIn **Companies**, of course! Here's an example of how to find companies according to your criteria.

In order to find a company in Dallas in the food and beverage industry, start an advanced search by clicking the magnifying glass symbol on the top navigation bar. Find "Food & Beverages" under the industry drop-down menu.

Next, choose your location by clicking **Lookup** under the Postal Code option. Type in Dallas to retrieve your postal code and then type it into the Postal Code field. After you hit **Search**, you'll notice that a few companies come up, one of which is the "Dr. Pepper Snapple Group". (The following visual displays these search results)

If you're having trouble coming up with companies for your list, don't forget that you can always conduct online research or, even better, talk to members of your career support network that work in those types of jobs and industries!

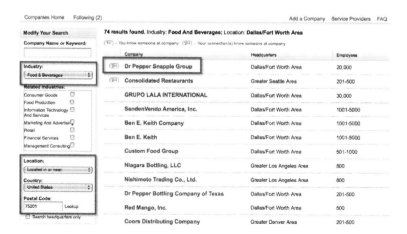

**I'VE CREATED MY TOP-TEN LIST...NOW WHAT?**

Once you've chosen your top ten companies, you're now ready to research them on LinkedIn to find out if you already have or can make any connections within them. At this point, your goal is to research the people within the organization so you can start to identify individuals of potential benefit. The next section will cover how you can use LinkedIn to research these people.

## 3. Research People

Earlier in this chapter, we told you that about 80 percent of the best jobs are located within the "hidden" job market. These career opportunities aren't advertised to the general public; rather, they're only accessible to those connected to the employer's network. The only way to tap into this network is to research people who can potentially connect you to the employer's key decision makers. In this section, we'll show you how to use LinkedIn to find and connect with key decision makers and potential champions within targeted companies and industries.

**RESEARCH PEOPLE IN TARGET COMPANIES**

Once you visit the company profile page of a target company, you should first view the current employees to see if you're already connected to anyone. Keep in mind you want to look beyond just first-degree connections; you also want to consider second and third-degree connections, those with whom you share a group, and finally LIONs — LinkedIn Open Networkers (we'll cover LIONs soon). Once you've determined how closely you're connected and through which person or group, decide the most appropriate way to make contact. Remember that different people are more comfortable making initial contact in different ways. This first interaction where you get to know each other is commonly referred to as an *informational interview*.

**INFORMATIONAL INTERVIEWS AND HOW TO ASK FOR THEM**

Throughout this book, we talk a lot about setting up meetings or informational interviews. An informational interview is an informal meeting with someone of influence. This person may, at some point, have the power to get you a job with their company or someone else's. This is an opportunity for you to learn about your target jobs, companies, and industries. It's also a chance for you to communicate what value you can add to an organization.

Recent Babson College graduate, Shirin Shahin, discovered how to use LinkedIn to locate people in her target companies and jobs so she could set up informational interviews:

"If I see a job posting, on any jobsite or search engine, I will go onto LinkedIn to see if I know anyone in my network who is at most a second-degree connection to me. There have been times when I have been able to find someone and arrange a phone conversation with this person in order to learn more about the company and their role."

How do you actually approach someone whom you'd like to set up an informational interview? Send them a LinkedIn message or email along these lines: "Hello Joshua. I saw your profile on LinkedIn and am interested in the work you did at Motorola. I am looking to find out more information on the company and wondered if you had about 20 minutes for me to ask about your experiences working there."

More often than not, the person will be happy to set up a meeting and share their knowledge and experiences with you. See more examples of how you can ask someone for an informational interview in the Appendix.

### TARGET THE HIRING MANAGER
The most powerful and effective way to get a job is to make direct contact with the final decision maker. In most companies, this is someone in Human Resources at the manager or director level. In smaller companies,

it may be the department manager or even the President or CEO. With that said, when you search the company profile for hiring managers, you should usually look for people with the following titles:

- Human Resource Director (or Manager)
- Talent Acquisition Director (or Manager)
- Recruiting Director (or Manager)
- Recruitment Director (or Manager)
- Corporate Recruiter
- Human Resource Generalist (or Specialist)

Now you may be asking yourself: how am I supposed to know who, of all these people, is the actual hiring manager? We don't actually expect you to know just by searching, but we also don't recommend using a "trial and error" approach. Be mindful of location (e.g. if you're looking for a job in Atlanta, don't contact someone in London) and look at job postings and the corporate website for clues to the hiring manager's identity.

WHAT IF I ACTUALLY FIND THE HIRING MANAGER?

In the event that you pinpoint the hiring manager on LinkedIn, investigate how closely connected you are to each other. If he or she is a first-degree connection (and you have a quality relationship), then by all means reach out to them. If they're a second-degree connection, look to see who of your first-degree connections would be most appropriate and willing to introduce you. If you share a group with the hiring manager, you already have the ability to send them a direct message via LinkedIn. In this case, we recommend you look at the **Contact Settings** at the bottom of their profile to confirm they are open to receiving job inquiries.

Hiring managers, however, are usually not the people who sort through resumes and spot potential candidates. Therefore, if you can't contact them directly, the next person you should look for on LinkedIn is the one responsible for searching for and screening applicants: the recruiter.

## FIND AND CONNECT WITH RECRUITERS

One of the best ways to stand out from a crowd of candidates is to find the recruiter before they have a chance to find you. As we said before, recruiters from some of the top companies are using LinkedIn to find candidates. When you visit the the profile page of one of your target companies, look for titles such as:

- Recruiter
- Recruiting Coordinator
- Recruitment Specialist
- Talent Acquisition Specialist
- Talent Specialist

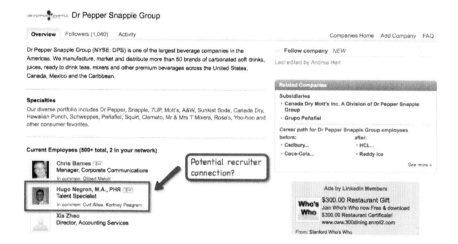

If you come across recruiters within the company profile, take the same approach you would for hiring managers. Be mindful of their title, location, and willingness to receive job inquiries. You might, however, find that many recruiters are a different breed of professional, and are quite open to connecting with you despite not having met you. This is because they're in the business of building a vast network of potential candidates and referral sources.

Before approaching recruiters on LinkedIn, it's important that you do your homework. For example, instead of sending them a message asking how the application process works and where to send your resume, find out that information yourself on the company website or in the job posting. Good ways to reach out to recruiters include:

- Asking intelligent questions about the company or career opportunities
- Requesting detailed information about the interviewing process
- Following up on your application or interview (assuming it is the right recruiter)
- Sending notes thanking them for their time and assistance throughout the recruiting process

### CONNECT WITH LIONS

When searching for people on LinkedIn, you may come across those referred to as LIONs or LinkedIn Open Networkers. This means they have a fairly wide open networking style and would be willing to add you as a connection without having known you previously. They are usually interested in building large and diverse networks. Whether or not you agree with this approach, there may be times where you should consider connecting with these individuals, especially in the event that they're recruiters for a company or industry you're interested in and you see potential of a Networlding relationship, of course!

### FIND AND CONNECT WITH CHAMPIONS

If you recall from "Expanding Your Career Support Network with LinkedIn", we provided a list of industry influencers who would make ideal members of your career support network. Here they are again:

- Corporate-level executives (i.e. CEO, VP)

- Mid-level managers or directors
- Key organizational or community decision makers
- Experienced working professionals
- Experts and knowledge leaders

Throughout your job search, it's possible that some of these individuals will serve as champions. *Champions* are people who are somehow connected to the company you're interested in applying to, and also have the ability to vouch, persuasively, for your cause. It's possible you may need to develop connections with new champions, depending on whether or not you already have connections to your target companies.

Champions are only champions, though, if they are open to helping you. That's why it is important to take the time to read their profiles to see just how active they are on LinkedIn and how they network. Active networkers on LinkedIn will tell you and show you through their profile what matters to them. Connect around the things that matter most to these people and you will create a much better first impression.

### RESEARCH CHAMPIONS IN YOUR TARGET COMPANIES AND INDUSTRIES

We hope we've made it clear in this book that the best time to create your career support network is before you actually need it. In the same manner, we recommend you find champions within the companies you're interested in pursuing well before you need a job. That way you have time to get to know each other well and build a quality relationship. Assuming you've done this, your connections will be more prepared to help you once it's time to pursue career opportunities. In this section, we'll include some tips on finding and leveraging champions within target companies and industries.

### MAXIMIZE COMPANY SEARCHES: LEARN ALL YOU CAN ABOUT THE COMPANY AND ITS CAREER OPPORTUNITIES

When you conduct company searches on LinkedIn, you're not just looking for hiring managers or recruiters. In fact, since they're responsible for finding reasons why they shouldn't hire you, consider reaching out to other employees inside the company. These individuals will be more likely to take the time to meet with you and share important information about the company and the job. This information can help prepare you for the interview, but can also provide a valuable validation test for your initial interest.

If you can, choose people who are within two degrees of you at the company, rather than three. With most companies you should be able to find these people through the **People Search** pages on LinkedIn. Identify those people who are in groups and then approach them with a request for an informational interview. Then use your interview to learn all you can about the company and its career opportunities now and, also, in the next thirty to ninety days.

Melissa notes that she has often seen job seekers find great opportunities by asking the question, "What jobs do you know of that might be coming up in the next thirty to ninety days?" This question often results in a job opening that has yet to become public, giving you a great edge on it before anyone else. In business this is called a first mover advantage and it's a great way to tap into the "hidden" job market.

RESEARCH MANAGERS AND EXECUTIVES

With that said, we recommend that you use the company profile to search for people who can provide the most accurate information about the company (e.g. culture, structure) or its job opportunities (e.g. positions, functions). The best people to target are those who have worked with the company for a long period of time and advanced to manager or executive levels. These individuals will provide the most accurate insights; they'll also be able to wield more influence on your behalf, if you build a meaningful relationship.

To find these people, visit the profile page of your target company and view all current employees. Don't forget to click **See more...** to scroll through all possible employees. This is where you'll look for people with managerial and executive-level job titles while also ascertaining how closely and in what way you are connected. You may also do the same for former employees because they may still have valuable information and experiences to share.

### RESEARCH PEOPLE WORKING IN YOUR TARGET JOB

Another type of person you should look for is someone actually working in the job or role you're interested in. Remember Chris Stewart? He was fortunate enough to get introduced to the person who used to have the job he was applying for. From his conversations with that person, he was able to get the inside scoop about the job.

To do this, search again through the current and former employees on the company profile, but this time look for people with job titles similar to what you're interested in doing.

Once you've found a potential champion, then what? Contact them to set up an informational interview, of course!

### MAXIMIZE PEOPLE SEARCH: LEARN WHAT IT TAKES TO BREAK INTO A COMPANY OR INDUSTRY

In the last section, we explained an approach to researching people within target companies using the **Companies** search option. Even though we recommend you research people within your top-ten target companies, we also realize that you may not have have a firm list in place yet. This is completely understandable. In this case, we suggest you pick out individuals who you aspire to be, and try to track their career path. Just remember that you don't have to follow anyone's career path exactly; they're just good examples. The following sections will show you how to maximize LinkedIn **People Search** to learn more about your own career path decisions.

FIND OUT WHERE PEOPLE WITH YOUR BACKGROUND ARE WORKING

One of the best ways to figure out where your career may be headed is to research people who have the skills, experience, and credentials you already have or plan to pursue. Find out where people with your desired background are working and what they are doing in their job. This can all be revealed by performing an **Advanced People Search** on LinkedIn.

Here's an example: let's say you're a finance major in your last year of college. You're interested in finding consultants in the financial industry so that you can learn more about what they do and what companies they work for in Chicago, where you plan to move after you graduate. Finally, your advisor recommends that you look into getting a Series 7 license because it will make you more marketable as a candidate.

The first thing you need to do is visit the **Advanced People Search** tab. Within the **Keywords** field, enter "series 7". Then under Location key in your Chicago zip code. Under **Industries**, check the **Financial Services** box and then hit **Search**. (See screen shot)

If you've made a conscious effort to build your career support network full of professionals in the finance industry, then you'll be more likely to come across profiles of people in the field. Look at all the resulting pro-files to get a sense of what companies these people are working for.

MORE ON RESEARCHING CAREER PATHS

We've already emphasized that a great way to find out what it takes to break into a company or industry is to research peoples' career paths. When you examine the profiles that came up in your search results, here are some questions to ask yourself:

- What school(s) is this professional attending and what were their majors and specializations?
- What type of degree did this person obtain? (e.g. Bachelor of Science, Master's degree)
- What additional certificates or licenses has this person received to move up in their career?
- What types of jobs did the person have immediately after they graduated from college or graduate school? (what were their job titles?)
- What types of companies and industries did this person work in prior to their current role?
- What LinkedIn groups are they a member of? (look for professional organizations and industry groups)
- What geographic locations seem to be common among the people you search for in a given industry?

By paying special attention to these details, you'll have a better idea of what path a person has taken to get where they are in their career. Since there's no one way to break into a field, you may want to research a large number of profiles. When you come across someone who seems interesting and you'd like to learn more about how they got where they are today, set up an informational interview.

The most successful strategy for Nick Farina was going through his groups and looking to connect with people who had similar interests, but were ahead of him in their careers. He knew he could learn things from their careers, and LinkedIn was a perfect place to study their career trajectories. He saw people who, like him, didn't have linear careers, but were successful. This was especially inspiring for Nick because he was an aspiring entrepreneur; he soon realized that everyone has their own unique path to success. We'll learn more about Nick's LinkedIn strategy in the next chapter.

## UNCOVER THE SECRET JOB REQUIREMENTS

While researching the profiles of professionals working in your field, there's a good chance you'll find people working in the types of positions you're looking for in your job search. In fact, this should be one of your goals when researching people on LinkedIn: to find people who are actually doing the work you aspire to do in your next job.

We would like to caution you, however, that job titles, and even job descriptions, can be misleading. A person's job title doesn't always represent what they actually do. In the same manner, what you read in a job posting may or may not tell you exactly what the job entails. Sometimes you need to hear about the job from someone who's actually in the role.

People working the same position you aspire to fill, or at least working together with that position, are the only ones who can tell you about the secret job requirements. The reality is that every company has unspoken qualities that they favor, and it seems many positions have unspoken responsibilities and duties. The only way to find these things out is by connecting to someone on the inside.

## MAXIMIZE GROUPS: LEARN FROM PEOPLE WHO ARE JUST ONE MESSAGE AWAY

We've talked a lot about the value of joining LinkedIn groups. We already know that groups are a great way to meet and connect with industry influencers, but they are also a great way to meet champions at the companies you want to work for.

When using LinkedIn to find potential champions who can help you get the job, don't forget about some of your key groups. If nothing else, make sure you tap into your school's alumni group. Also consider researching the profiles of people in your professional organization and industry groups. And again, once you find someone who could serve as a potential champion, set up an informational interview. Remember that since you share a group with this person, LinkedIn allows you to send them a message directly without needing an introduction.

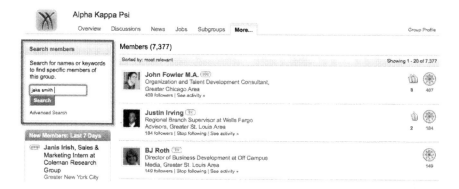

You can also perform targeted searches for people within these groups. Do this by visiting the home page of a group, clicking on the **More...** link and selecting **Members**. This allows you to scroll through and view profiles for all the members of this group. Take your search within this group to the next level by using the **Search Members** feature (shown above). For example, type the name of one of your target companies and you'll see which group members have that company on their profile.

## 4. Find Jobs

We've been emphasizing that in order to conduct a successful job search, it's wise to focus more on companies and people, not just jobs. What makes this approach effective is that it allows you to tap into the "hidden" job market, uncovering some of the best career opportunities not known to the general public. We are not, however, suggesting that you totally ignore jobs listed on Monster.com or other job search engines. We're not telling you to avoid searching company websites for job openings. People do find jobs by applying to online postings.

What we *are* suggesting: if the job posting is where you start, then the next place you should go is LinkedIn to increase your chances of getting that job.

If you decide to search for jobs online, there are a wide variety of websites you can visit. Here's a list of what we consider to be the top job search engines:
• LinkedIn (of course!)
• Monster.com
• Indeed.com
• USA.gov
• CareerBuilder
• Dice
• LinkUp
• Yahoo Hot Jobs
• SimplyHired
• Craigslist

Once you come across a desirable job posting, the first thing you should be thinking is: how can I get an edge on being considered for this job? Then think about how you can utilize the strategies in this book to research the companies and then the people who can help you get the job.

Earlier, we mentioned that the first place Lauren goes when she finds a job posting is LinkedIn. She conducts a **Companies** Search to see who she knows on the inside who might be able to help get her resume to the right person.

Amber Sharma takes a similar approach. As a student of The Catholic School of America, she leveraged the LinkedIn **Companies** Search to get the names and contact information of hiring managers whom she could send her resume directly. She also researched the interviewer's profile so she could get a "leg up" in the interview process. Lauren and Amber both set an exemplary precedent for succeeding with LinkedIn.

## HOW TO USE LINKEDIN JOBS

The great thing about LinkedIn is that it also serves as a job search engine. As the job seeker, you can search for job opportunities while simultaneously leveraging inside connections. Hiring managers also benefit by tapping into LinkedIn's massive network of ideal candidates.

Searching for jobs on LinkedIn is easy. Simply click on the **Jobs** link on the top navigation tool bar. The home page of **Jobs** gives you the option to perform a simple keyword search within a specific geographic location, or you can conduct a more advanced search by selecting the **Advanced Search** link or tab. Just like the **People Search** and **Companies** features, you can search according to keywords and certain criteria. Search jobs according to the following criteria:

- Location
- Experience level
- Date posted
- Title
- Company
- Job function
- Industry

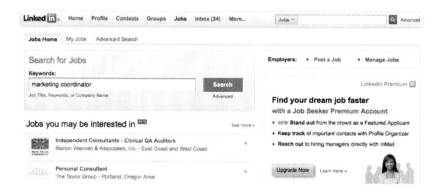

FINDING AND APPLYING FOR JOBS ON LINKEDIN

Jobs that match your search terms and filtering criteria will be returned in two clickable tabs:

- LinkedIn Jobs: positions posted directly on LinkedIn, including exclusive listings
- The Web: positions from partner sites all over the web (including the search engines we listed above)

Regardless of the source, LinkedIn will display who in your network can help you with this position, quickly and easily connecting you to potential champions. Like we've stated throughout this chapter, help may come in the form of learning about the company, learning about the position, or even getting introduced to the hiring manager.

Once you've returned search results, if you'd like to expand or refine your query, check the **Keep refine selections** box and make changes without losing the information you've already entered.

Applying for a job is as easy as clicking the **Apply Now** button on the specific job listing page and filling in a few pieces of information. Information you provide during the application process along with your LinkedIn profile will be sent to the job poster.

Another thing that makes searching for jobs on LinkedIn so powerful is the way it allows you to instantly see who in your career support network connects you to the job poster (See the screen shot above). You can request an introduction, which your connection will hopefully choose to accept and then serve as your champion.

See a job that isn't for you, but could be a perfect fit for one of your classmates? LinkedIn allows you to forward job postings to people in your career support network. Simply click the **Forward job** link and pass it along for their consideration. You may just help someone in your network launch their dream career. If you think this couldn't happen to you or someone you know, think again.

Marie Bjornson, recent master's graduate of The Chicago School of Professional Psychology, had been looking for jobs in career coaching. The problem was, she was working full-time in a small consulting firm while, at the same time, pursuing her coaching certification. This schedule didn't allow much extra time for a full-blown job search effort. So what did she do?

Marie started becoming more vocal about her professional brand. She reached out to her most trusted connections, those within her primary circle, and clearly communicated what types of opportunities she was targeting in her quest to jump-start her coaching career. Then one day, she received an email from a former classmate that read, "Marie, I found this job on LinkedIn and thought you might be interested. It looks like it's right up your alley."

Of course, Marie immediately applied because her connection was right. The job *was* exactly what she was looking for. After two interviews and less than two months later, Marie was showing up for her first day on the job:

"I shared with my network that I was actively seeking a career services position, and that I was certified as a career coach. One of them found a 'Career Readiness Coach' position at a school in downtown Chicago through the 'LinkedIn Job Search' function, and sent it to me directly through LinkedIn. Now I've landed my dream job and couldn't be happier!"

Marie is living proof that LinkedIn can be a powerful means to finding the right job, especially when it's used in conjuction with the wonderful of approach to building relationships — the Networlding approach to LinkedIn.

### DISCOVER JOBS IN LINKEDIN GROUPS

At this point, it's no surprise that LinkedIn Jobs is a valuable tool for finding career opportunities. However, we also want to encourage you to take another approach to job searching: tap into LinkedIn **Groups** as well.

Steven Silverman, recent graduate of the University of Michigan at Dearborn, managed to get an interview for a job that he found within one of his recruiting groups. He simply visited his group on LinkedIn and clicked the tab labeled **Jobs**. Mitchell McKenna also attributes his success in landing an interview to LinkedIn **Groups**. This recent graduate was ecstatic when he found he could search for postings within the very industry groups he joined while building his career support network. He realized that he didn't have to rely on just the traditional job search engines like CareerBuilder and Monster.com to uncover opportunities.

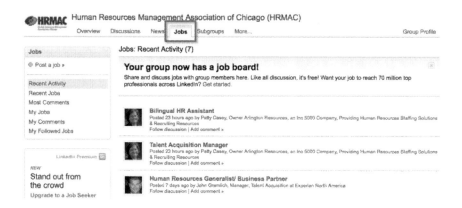

What's more, the **Jobs** tab within **Groups** allows you to make *comments* about the position, getting you in direct contact with the person who posted the job (which most likely is the recruiter). This is a great opportunity to interact with them and ask questions about the job and application process. You can also *follow* these job postings in the same way that you're able to follow discussions. This helps you track the activity within the posting and follow up on any comments you might have made.

After Steven discovered a job within his recruiting group, he immediately jumped on the opportunity and applied through LinkedIn. But once he found out he had secured an interview, was he now done using LinkedIn? Absolutely not. The next section will explain how he, among several other students, used LinkedIn to get an edge on the interview process.

### USING LINKEDIN TO PREPARE FOR THE INTERVIEW

Just because you finally landed that job interview doesn't mean you're done with LinkedIn. In the same way you used LinkedIn to research potential connections, industry influencers, or champions, you can also use it to research those who will be interviewing you for your next job. Of all the strategies we've discussed thus far, this seems to be one of the most widely used by college and graduate students alike.

Here's how Steven Silverman used LinkedIn to look up his interviewer's profile:

"Before the first interview, I was able to look up my interviewer's profile, which told me something about the person on the other side of the phone. I found out where he went to school, how many people he supervises, and how long he has been working for the company. Now I can do the same with my second interviewer."

Remember Heather Pollock? Before she landed her job as an HR Analyst, she researched the interviewer by performing a simple **People Search** on LinkedIn:

"I believe it is important to know your audience for any presentation, and I view interviews as exactly that. While preparing for my interviews, I utilized LinkedIn as a research tool to understand my audience's professional backgrounds. LinkedIn makes this time-honored interview technique simple with its easy search abilities and resume-like profiles. In other words, it gives you quick access to anyone's job history and a depiction of their career progression. I quickly located those listed on my interview agenda by simply entering their names and the company, took a few notes on professional achievements for each of my interviewers and learned what topics they have expertise in. This helped tremendously as I interviewed. Not only was I able to demonstrate my talents relative to their professional experiences, but I was able to highlight a few strengths I had that matched the job, demonstrating how they might also grow in knowledge through our partnership. Needless to say, my interviews were successful and I was offered the job."

And then there's Adam Carson, MBA student at the Tuck School of Business at Dartmouth. He thinks he got his job largely due to interviewer research on LinkedIn. In his research he discovered that the interviewer was, in fact, a second-degree connection through a person he knew within the company. In turn, the person Adam knew put in a good word for him. Upon meeting Adam at the interview, the first thing the interviewer said was "How do you know Bill?" And from that question, an informal conversation began that put Adam at ease and allowed him to build rapport with the interviewer.

What these stories demonstrate is this: just by doing a little research on LinkedIn, you can make that first meeting or phone call so much easier. As we've found, the information you glean from a person's profile can be quite powerful, especially when it helps you find points of commonality with the people responsible for putting you in that first job upon graduation. If you take only one thing away from this book, take this strategy and use it prior to meeting anyone, whether they're potential networking partners, industry influencers, sales leads, or newfound champions.

# Using LinkedIn Beyond Graduation

# CHAPTER 8

# Using LinkedIn Beyond Graduation

If you've reached this chapter, you have hopefully learned how to build a career support network that can help you get your career underway. Perhaps you will use LinkedIn to find a mentor or maybe use it to get an interview for an internship or job. But it's not just about getting jobs; LinkedIn is also a great tool for people who aren't job hunting. In this concluding chapter, we'll provide you with some tips to whet your appetite and get you thinking about ways you can use LinkedIn in your job or as an entrepreneur.

Consider John Exley, current student at Clarkson University in New York. John was only in his third year of college when he established his professional brand on LinkedIn.

This rising star not only studied abroad at National University in Singapore, but he has also worked with an exciting Chicago-based start-up that specializes in multimedia personal and professional development. As blogger and host of an emerging leader interview series, John provided promotional support by creating captivating content that brought value to and promoted additional traffic to the company's website and community. He talked about Generation Y, networking, college leadership development, and start-ups. Now he's interning with a leading technology company as a social media marketing specialist. John clearly understands the power behind a robust professional brand:

"As far as brandbuilding, I think the best thing has been that recruiters, friends, people I'm just meeting, people who are about to interview me, future customers, or anyone who is just 'researching' me is able to go the extra mile beyond my resume because I go further in detail on LinkedIn than my resume allows, and thus the external evaluator is able to see what I actually accomplished in different roles."

This college student also realizes that LinkedIn profiles (online professional brands) work the other way around. He finds LinkedIn quite useful for finding people to interview for his work as a blogger:

"I was preparing to interview Ming Yong, the CEO and Co-Founder of a Singapore-based company. Best page to begin my research on his career? LinkedIn, hands down. Right there I had a digestable story of his whole career. His school, former jobs and startups, the fact that he had 500+ connections, and his recommendations. I had a paragraph description from his Co-Founder right at my fingertips describing his personality. I had his blog too. Because of LinkedIn and the knowledge it gave me of his past, I was in a much better position to ask questions in the interview."

Or take Nick Farina, for example. Nick is a recent graduate of Haverford College and visiting student at the University of Oxford in the United Kingdom. As you can tell by his LinkedIn profile summary, entrepreneurship is nothing less of a way of life for Nick. Not only is he founder of One Step Auction, but also he is starting a new business called Money in English.

Nick is using LinkedIn to reach his target audience (18 – 25 years) and help them understand and manage their finances. Not only that, he wants to show them how to make money and succeed in their careers:

"A big part of what I'm working on is not just how to manage your money but also how to make money — how to get a job and how to get a promotion. And LinkedIn will be a big part of that. For example, having a database is so important for building your career. And business cards, while essential when you first meet someone, can only go so far. With LinkedIn, you can see what someone has been up to recently, learn about their past, their interests, etc… And that's how, next time you meet them, you can find common ground and build a real relationship."

---

**Nick Farina** (1·)

Director at e-Conversation

Greater Chicago Area | Consumer Services

| Current | • **Director at e-Conversation** |
|---------|----------------------------------|
| | • **Principal at Money in English** |
| | • **Screenwriter at Kabazzle** |
| Past | • Founder at One Step Auction |
| Education | • Haverford College |
| | • University of Oxford |
| Recommendations | **3 people have recommended Nick** |
| Connections | 442 connections |
| Websites | • My Company |
| | • My Articles |
| Public Profile | http://www.linkedin.com/in/nickfarina |

---

## Summary

Entrepreneurship is a lifestyle for me; I don't think anything is more exciting than building a company or finding fresh ideas to solve a problem. In 2003, I founded one of the first eBay drop-off companies, and later expanded that into a specialized inventory liquidation service.

Currently, I am a Director and founding team member at e-Conversation Solutions, the only company to create and produce search-optimized video for businesses.

I'm also working on Money in English, which is the one-stop source for young adults to learn the basics of personal finance. I maintain a blog - which is currently being redesigned into a full-featured website - and serve as the director of the City of Chicago Treasurer's Youth Personal Finance Initiative.

My other love is screenwriting. I have written four feature-length scripts, and am interested in any dramatic writing opportunities. I have writing samples available upon request.

I serve on the Advisory Boards of the Financial Management Institute and the Networking Innovation Center, and write a weekly column on entrepreneurship for Alrroya.

### Specialties

Personal Finance, Inventory Liquidation, Screenwriting

As you can see, both John and Nick have already realized how LinkedIn can help them be more productive at work or even launch and run a business. Perhaps what's most important (and impressive) is how they've been able to adhere to the Networlding approach to LinkedIn.

For example, John started building his professional brand on LinkedIn early in college. As a result, he is easily found by potential members of his career support network (e.g. recruiters, industry influencers, mentors) and he has been able to cultivate solid working relationships with them. In the same manner, Nick has already discovered as a college student how he can use LinkedIn as a tool for making meaningful connections with his potential customers — it's about quality, not quantity and giving, not just taking:

"I find that LinkedIn is most valuable for building relationships, and not just for adding sheer numbers. Right now I have about 400 connections, but I have interacted personally with each and every one of them. And that's what's important — those are the people who I can help, and who can help me when I need it."

Now if those two aren't Networlders, then we don't know who is!

At this point, it should be evident that most of the success stories in this book might not have taken place if it wasn't for LinkedIn and the process we call Networlding. As we stated in the "Foreward", there's a good chance this book would not exist if it wasn't for the power of social media and LinkedIn. Beyond using LinkedIn to establish the relationship, John and Melissa have both used it to complete this book, therefore, we'd like to share with you five strategies for leveraging LinkedIn in your jobs like John Exley and Nick Farina do.

# Five Strategies for Using LinkedIn in Your Job and in Business

Whether you are trying to be more effective in your job, promoting someone's products or services, or launching your own business, LinkedIn should be your go-to resource. We'd like to present you with five of our top strategies for using LinkedIn beyond life as a student, just to get you thinking about how it can be used once you've entered the world of work.

### Find Customers, Clients, and Partners

In this book we showed you how to use LinkedIn to find and connect with industry influencers, mentors — simply anyone who has the potential to help you succeed in your career. Well, the same rules apply when helping a business grow and prosper.

Use LinkedIn **People Search** to target those who might be interested in you or your company's offerings. Better yet, leverage **Companies** to look for the people who influence the buying decisions (i.e. key decision makers) and see if you share a connection and can get introduced. Or use LinkedIn to look for individuals who might want to collaborate with you on a project or organizations which might serve as good business partners.

### Promote Your Company or Business

Just as LinkedIn gives you a profile to showcase your qualifications and communicate your professional brand, it also does the same for companies. Try using the **Companies** feature to find your company's profile. Company profiles are a great marketing tool because they give companies the chance to provide key information about their products or services. Better yet, they usually include a link to the company website. This link helps drive traffic (people) to the website and increase the chances visitors will take the time to learn about the company and its offerings. If you are starting your own business, consider creating a profile that includes a link to your website.

Another way to promote your company or business is by including website links within status updates. For example, let's say you work for PepsiCo and they have just released a new soft drink. Your status update may say something like "PepsiCo launches sweet new diet drink" and you follow this statement with a link to the PepsiCo website page with information about the product. You can do the same with your business. When providing updates, include a link to your website or, better yet, to your blog.

### Engage your audience

What good does it do to promote your company or business by relying on one-way communication? Don't you care what your customers think about you or your company's offerings?

Just as we encourage you to use LinkedIn **Groups** (Discussions Forum) and **Answers** to converse and connect with potential career support members, the same goes for companies. Initiating and participating in discussions on LinkedIn is a wise way to solicit and monitor feedback about you or your company's brand. Aside from that, **Groups** and status updates are great avenues for sharing information with your audience about news, best practices, and industry trends.

### Keep Up with the Happenings in Your Industry

Speaking of industry trends, one of the best ways to keep up with the happenings in your industry is to engage in conversations with industry influencers and knowledge leaders in **Groups** and **Answers**. Are you starting to catch on to the value of discussions forums for the purpose of learning, sharing, and connecting?

Don't forget about your LinkedIn home page! If you've set this as your browser's home page, then you will receive real-time updates from your network about what's going on with your groups, the companies you're following, and any other goings-on within your network. Remember how

Maria got a job in Spain just by responding to the status update of the hiring manager she interviewed with? Pay attention to people's status updates! Whether you are running your own business or working for an organization, it's very important to stay informed about what's happening in your field.

## Continue to Grow and Nurture Your Network

If for any reason you feel that the LinkedIn tips we've covered are not relevant to your job or business, then at least hear us out regarding our next and final point. Just because you've landed a lucrative job or you're running a thriving busines, you never know when you might need support from your network, especially in the current economy. That's why we encourage you to continue growing and nuturing the relationships you've established, no matter how good you feel about your career.

## Final Thoughts

Hopefully our advice in tandem with these examples is enough to convince you that LinkedIn isn't just a one-year game you should play your last year of college, it's an amazing tool that you can use to facilitate a whole new way of networking: Networlding!

Whether you're on the job hunt, in the midst of the interview process, or well established in your career, it's never too late to graduate to LinkedIn. We wish you the best of luck!

# Appendix

# Appendix

## Take the Networlding Quiz

| Questions | NEVER 1 | SELDOM 2 | OCASSIONALLY 3 | OFTEN 4 | ALWAYS 5 |
|---|---|---|---|---|---|
| 1. Believe it is important to make a difference | | | | | |
| 2. Believe that anything is possible | | | | | |
| 3. Believe you are guided by strong inner beliefs, intent or principles | | | | | |
| 4. Believe you create your own rewards | | | | | |
| 5. Believe you can get anything done through others | | | | | |
| 6. Believe people are your most creative resource | | | | | |
| 7. Share your goals with others | | | | | |
| 8. Build/nurture relationships with those who can help you achieve your goals | | | | | |
| 9. Limit relationships with selfish individuals and those that don't help you realize your goals | | | | | |
| 10. Respect the creative process and are result/outcome focused | | | | | |
| 11. Believe that Networlding/ Networking shortens the time to get things done | | | | | |
| 12. Assume that Networlding/ Networking is a balanced process of giving and receiving | | | | | |

| | | | | | |
|---|---|---|---|---|---|
| 13. Believe Networlding/ Networking can provide all needed resources to reach your goals | | | | | |
| 14. When Networlding/ Networking you ask for what you want | | | | | |
| 15. When Networlding/ Networking you discover others' interests and needs | | | | | |
| 16. When Networlding/ Networking you expect to discover/create new opportunities | | | | | |
| 17. Networld/ Network with influential people who can make things happen | | | | | |
| 18. Offer emotional, information and other support to your Networld/ Network partners | | | | | |
| 19. Respond quickly to the requests and needs of your Networld/ Network partners | | | | | |
| 20. Measure the results of your Networlding/ Networking efforts | | | | | |

Total Your Score: _____ *Novice (Score: 20-44) Networker (Score: 45-64)*
*Strategic Networker (Score: 65-84) Networlding Expert (Score: 85-100)*

## Examples for Sending Messages to Connections on LinkedIn
### Inviting someone to connect

Hi Chetan,

It was great to meet you at the fundraising event on Tuesday. I enjoyed learning about how you got started in the field of finance and real estate. I'd like to connect with you on LinkedIn so we can keep in touch and share information and opportunities.

Sincerely,
Jacqueline

Dear Susan,

I'm glad we were able to chat over the phone today. I enjoyed every bit of our conversation, especially as it related to our passions for mentoring and best practices in corporate and academia. Please let me know if I can ever be of assistance. I hope our paths cross again soon.

David

## Requesting an Introduction
## Your message to Dr. Canfield (person to whom you'd like to be introduced)

Hi Dr. Canfield,

I am a senior bioengineering student at Northwestern University in Chicago; I'm currently in the midst of a research project and I noticed from your LinkedIn profile that you have considerable experience in preclinical testing in animals. I would love the opportunity to learn about your previous research approaches. Would you be willing to speak over the phone? Thanks for your time and consideration.

Jacob

## Your brief note to your connection (person from whom you are requesting the introduction)

Hello Steven,

I hope things are going well with the consulting gig. I'm doing this huge research project about animal testing and noticed you are connected to Dr. Melanie Canfield, who has a lot of experience in this area. Would you be willing to introduce me to her provided you know her well and feel comfortable doing so?

Jacob

## Requesting a Recommendation (endorsement)

Hey Kavita,

I was wondering if you could write a brief recommendation for me on LinkedIn. I enjoyed working on the homecoming project and marketing campaign with you last year. I was hoping you could speak to my leadership skills as President of Sigma Kappa. Please let me know if you have any questions. I would really appreciate this!

Janice

Hi Sid,

Would you be willing to write a three or four sentence recommendation regarding my work as your marketing intern last summer? I can't express how valuable this experience was to me — I'm so proud we were able to roll out the campaign successfully. If you have any questions about the endorsement, please let me know. Thanks!

Terence

## Writing a Recommendation (endorsement)

Authentic, loyal, dedicated, and strong-willed. These words are just the "tip of the iceberg" when I think of the nature of Sarah's professional demeanor. As a co-worker at Axiom Consulting, she showed me how to take a non-conventional approach to problem solving. As my Co-President of the I/O Task Force, Sarah taught me the value of making unpopular decisions in order to ensure long-term growth and success of a young organization. Last but not least, as a graduate student and rising star in the field of I/O Psychology, Sarah consistently demonstrated above par consulting skills. She is hands-down one of the most active listeners and most confident decision-makers I've met thus far. It's been great working with Sarah in every capacity. She is surely a unique and strong asset to any organization looking for a leader who is fully capable of eliciting change and making an impact.

As a mentor, Jonathan gave me the educational, professional, and social support I needed to take my graduate school career to the next level. As my classmate, he consistently brought quality business expertise and solid dedication to his projects. Jonathan is an authentic consultant and coach who serves as a great example for colleagues, peers, supervisors, and clients alike. I highly recommend him for your individual or organizational performance needs.

### Requesting an Informational Interview from an industry influencer

Hi Frank,

It was great chatting with you at the conference last week.  Since then, I've been researching more about your company and the opportunities you offer in operations management. As Operations Manager of Smith Company, I imagine you might have some advice regarding what it takes to succeed in your job function. Would you be willing to meet with me next week and discuss your work with Smith Company? Let me know your thoughts. Thanks!

Ravi

Silvia,

Congratulations on your recent success with the art show. Your style of painting has truly inspired me to challenge what I'm learning in school. Although I am making progress academically, I am still unsure about how I will go about opening up my own gallery — the business side is not one of my strengths. Would you be willing to grab lunch or coffee within the next couple of weeks? I'd love to learn about how you got where you are today.

Rebecca

# Other Networlding Tools for Your Career Success

*Networlding: Building Relationships and Opportunities for Success*
Melissa Giovagnoli Wilson and Jocelyn-Carter Miller
**http://budurl.com/NetworldingBook1**

The book that started it all. Here are the original reviews by Amazon and Publishers Weekly:

### Amazon.com Review

If "networking" was the battle cry of the business world at the tail end of the 20th century, Melissa Giovagnoli Wilson and Jocelyn Carter-Miller hope to make "Networlding" its call to arms in the new millennium. Giovagnoli, a consultant and speaker, and Carter-Miller, a Motorola executive, agree that one-to-one connectivity is still the key to professional advancement. However, they believe their updated concept will prove more effective in coming years because, if properly implemented, it will forge deeper bonds and lead to greater opportunities than its more superficial predecessor ever could. In *Networlding*, the authors explain their practice as a "purposeful process of collaboration" among individuals who "share similar intent, values, goals, and interests." They then lay out a seven-step system for developing such mutually beneficial personal relationships, ranging from the establishment of "a values-rich foundation" through the formation and cultivation of a circle of "connections" with whom you "co-create opportunities" that move everyone ahead. There are plenty of specifics, exercises, and real-life examples here for those serious about attempting this technique. It should prove applicable for almost anyone in any type of business situation and virtually any stage of his or her career. — **Howard Rothman**

## From Publishers Weekly

Declaring that in today's workplace, simple networking is no longer enough, Giovagnoli and Carter-Miller present a prescriptive plan combining career advancement with social reform. In contrast to the traditional aim of networking for one's own financial gain or prestige, they espouse "Networlding," in which advancement may be a motive but there's a difference in intent. Networlding involves focusing on a larger issue, such as increasing diversity in the workplace or offering assistance for a social program. Among the specific rules of Networlding offered by Giovagnoli, a human resource specialist, and Carter-Miller, an executive at Motorola: "Grow and nurture your relationships," "Expand your connections" and "Make both your redundant and divergent connections count." The last rule is easy to overlook: the authors cite someone looking for a job who got a lead after talking to a parent at a Little League game. Even more important than following these rules is having a clear sense of one's values. The authors present a straightforward approach for identifying and prioritizing values, creating a personal charter and setting goals for the coming year. While readers who haven't consciously networked during their career may find this approach difficult to follow, those who have will benefit from this concise and innovative primer.

*The Nanosecond Networlders: Changing Lives in An Instant Forever*
Melissa Giovagnoli Wilson and David Stover

http://budurl.com/NanoNetworldersBook

Do you wish to surround yourself with people of like-minded values but struggle to find them? Are you experiencing a variety of 'takers' in your life, and spending all your energies defending yourself or your department or your company? *The Nanosecond Networlders* show us that there are compelling new solutions to some of the most vexing cross-cultural, career, and organizational business issues we face today. These solutions recognize that every decision is made in a split-second, and that although we often deliberate for months, the moment of commitment is the moment that counts. Making that commitment in a way that is firmly rooted in recognized individual core values is the key. No one can remove those barriers alone. This book shows us how to participate in an 'exchange' of ideas, values, and solutions to break through to our true potential — by leveraging the limitless possibilities inherent in every conversation we have.

*Networlding Guidebook: Building Strategic Relationships Through Networking*
Melissa Giovagnoli
http://budurl.com/NetworldingGuidebook

Networlding Guidebook: The Networlding Guidebook is designed as a companion to author Melissa Giovagnoli's bestselling book Networlding. While the first book provided an introduction to the overall concepts and practices of Networlding, this guidebook is intended to help you put Networlding into motion in real-time. Filled with checklists, questions and exercises to help you assess where you are in terms of your networks and the goals you hope to achieve through the implementation of Networlding, as well as a month-by-month action plan to roll out the process, The Networlding Guidebook is a fun, practical and easy-to-understand resource that helps you transform relationships from a pipeline of opportunities to a lifeline in our new world of work.
http://budurl.com/NetworldingGuidebook

# About the Authors

Melissa is one of the world's leading experts in the development of networks as a means of growing and accelerating brand loyalty, growing new markets, creating new products and building thought leadership. She is also the founder of Networlding, a firm specializing in social network innovation. Her clients have included organizations such as Motorola, Hewitt, Office Depot, BF Goodrich, AT&T, American Express, Medtronic, CNA, UBS and hundreds of emerging companies.

Innovating in the social media and social networking space, the firm helps organizations: grow thought leadership, build digital trust, grow markets, manage their online presence and integrate social media with their other marketing initiatives. One the most innovative strategies the firm offers is book and e-book publishing.

Melissa is also the author and/or co-author of 11 top-selling books. Her seventh book, co-authored with former CMO of Office Depot, Jocelyn Carter Miller, held the #10 spot on Amazon (in Chicago) for a year.

**Her other books include:**

*Networlding: Building Relationships and Opportunities for Success* —
**#10 on Amazon, in Chicago, for 12 months**

*The Chicago Entrepreneurs Sourcebook* — **rated one of the top 10 small business books in Chicago**

*75 Cage Rattling Questions that Change the Way You Work* — McGraw Hill
*The Power of Two: Rethinking and Reforming Strategic Alliances* — Jossey Bass

Four of Melissa's books have been on top business book lists. Additionally, *The Power of Two and Networlding*, were named by Booz Allen as two of the top ten alliance management books.

Melissa has also been a guest on both radio and television including The Today Show, CNN, WGN, CNBC and FOX. One of her books was featured on The Oprah Winfrey Show. She has been professionally speaking for fifteen years and has won a Consummate Speaker of the Year Award.

With a B.A. in Sociology and a J.D. from DePaul University College of Law, Melissa went on to found Service Showcase, Inc., a management consulting and training firm. In 2000, she started Networlding to include the work she pioneered in social networks. In 1998 she was named one of "The Six Outstanding Women of the Decade" chosen by The University of Chicago Women's Graduate Business Alumni Board. The Networlding licensing product she created has been licensed by Yale University through their graduate school of business as well as Motorola University and is currently being sold to organizations and non-profits around the world.

She has used LinkedIn since it started, helping thousands of executives over the past seven years learn to harness the power of a site she believes is the best thing that has happened for professional networking.

John Fowler is an emerging leader in organization and talent development consulting. With a unique blend of business and psychology expertise, he helps companies and individuals realize and maximize human potential, talent, and connection.

After obtaining his B.S. in Marketing from the University of Missouri – Columbia in 2002, John later went on to pursue his master's from The Chicago School of Professional Psychology. In 2008, he established himself as an independent consultant focused on producing, refining, and facilitating organization talent processes, programs, and tools. With in-depth knowledge with and a passion for social networks, his most recent work includes delivering LinkedIn networking and job-hunting training to students and young professionals; he also advises business leaders on formulating and implementing social media marketing strategies and helps functional experts use LinkedIn to enhance productivity. John's clients have included individuals within Chicago-based universities such as DePaul and Argosy. Additionally, he has consulted with small IT and management consulting firms as well as large corporations such as Leo Burnett and CareerBuilder.

John started using LinkedIn to source talent as a recruiter in 2006. Since then he has used it religiously for his own business and professional development. Like Melissa, most of his recent work has been devoted to educating, engaging, and empowering students and business leaders about its amazing power and potential.

# Stay in Touch!

We want to encourage you to stay in touch with us. That's why we formed a group on LinkedIn called **"Graduate to LI: Grow Your Career Support Network Now."** It's a place where we will continue to share best practices on LinkedIn and beyond into the best social media tools we can offer that integrate well with LinkedIn.

You can also follow us on **Twitter (@GradtoLinkedIn)** and become a fan on Facebook.

**We also welcome you to email either of us:**
**GraduateToLinkedInTheBook@gmail.com.** Share us your best LinkedIn success stories and if we use one of them for upcoming updates to this book, we'll be sure to give you credit and therefore help you grow your influence! You can also use our emails to link with us on LinkedIn.

Finally, we speak on the subject of LinkedIn and social media/social networking and welcome communication from any of you who want to see us speak at your college. Feel free to contact us for that purpose.

# Speaking

John and Melissa are available for speaking at your college or organization. To contact John, email him directly at **john.ray.fowler@gmail.com**. To contact Melissa directly, email her at at **melissa@Networlding.com**.

# Special Last Note

Melissa and John are committed to helping younger people get what they call "Smart Starts" in their careers. To this end half of all the proceeds from this book will go to initiatives that help 12 – 29 year olds improve their chances of success in the world.

Made in the USA
Lexington, KY
22 July 2013